TRAVEL

FOR

FREE

HOW TO USE POINTS AND
MILES TO SEE THE WORLD

by

JASON STEELE

Published by Leadership Books, Inc.
Las Vegas, Nevada – New York, New York

LeadershipBooks.com

ISBN:
Hardback: 978-1-965401-24-8
Paperback: 978-1-965401-25-5
eBook: 978-1-965401-26-2

Leadership Books, Inc is committed to publishing works of quality and integrity. In that spirit, we are proud to offer this book to our readers; however, the story, the experiences, and the words are the authors alone. The conversations in the book all come from the author's recollections, not word-for-word transcripts. All of the events are true to the best of the author's memory. The author, in no way, represents any company, corporation, or brand mentioned herein. The views expressed are solely those of the author.

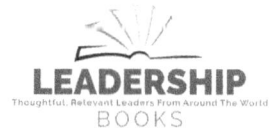

ACKNOWLEDGMENTS

I'm not smart enough to come up with the idea for free travel by myself, but rather I've drawn on the inspiration of others, whose work I have admired for close to 20 years now. In my view, the giants of the field are Randy Peterson, who is credited with creating the FlyerTalk online travel forums and BoardingArea.com, which is a collection of travel blogs; and Brian Kelly, who is the founder of ThePointsGuy.com. This site, which I've been honored to contribute to since 2012, has inspired millions to live vicariously through Kelly's travels and to learn about the wonderful world of Award Travel.

But even before The Points Guy, there were my parents — Jane and Cliff Steele — who originally inspired my love of travel and taught me to always add my frequent flier number to every airline reservation.

I would also like thank the editorial team at Leadership Books for tirelessly examining the minutiae of my manuscript and helping me translate my travel nerd-speak into English whenever I devolved into that mode of writing.

And finally, I have to thank my wife, Janna, who stuffed her purse with credit cards and put up with my travel rewards obsession, even when others had dismissed it as pointless fantasy.

CONTENTS

INTRODUCTION

One day in 2013, I came home from work and asked my wife if we wanted to take the family on a vacation to Hawaii during our kids' spring break. Instead of replying with an enthusiastic "Yes!," she instead complained that we had been traveling too much. Her response was fair, as we had already taken several vacations in the past year, having recently discovered how to earn and spend travel rewards points and miles.

"Look," I contended, "I can get us a non-stop flight to Maui in first class, and we can stay at the Hyatt Regency." She ultimately relented and we had a great time. But I frequently think of this experience to remind myself just how fortunate we are to be able to travel as often as we wish. I mean, I actually had to convince my wife to take a vacation to Hawaii! And because we paid for all of the airfare and hotels with points and miles, the cost was negligible. All we had to have was the time and desire to travel.

What would your life look like, if like me, your travel was limited only by your available time, and not your money?

This is an important question. And as an expert in award travel, I often ask the individuals and small business owners I consult with how their life would be different if they could take advantage of the unlimited travel opportunities that are available to award travel enthusiasts. Over the years, as I've worked with numerous friends, family members and clients, I've witnessed that learning how to travel for free will not just save you money but will actually change your life. Award travel can be so much more than just fun trips to sunny places. Having the ability to travel for free with points and miles brings you closer to your family members and friends across the country and around the world. These face-to-face connections in real life will allow you to relate to people and places in ways that are impossible to duplicate online. You can build strong relationships with friends around the country and strengthen out-of-town business partnerships. And distant relatives can become people you don't just see at weddings and funerals, but an important part of your life.

To illustrate just how much low-cost to no-cost travel can change your life, I love to tell the story of my cousin Lorraine. Before retirement, she and her husband and son lived in New York City. As long as I could remember I would only see them at family occasions every few years, and frankly we weren't particularly close.

When she heard that my family had been traveling a lot and that we were doing so for little to no cost, she was eager to learn more. I was happy to teach her about award travel, and she eventually began implementing—with enthusiasm   the things I had taught her. As she later put it to me in a letter, "I used to travel three times a year, once to see my father in Florida, once for a family vacation, and once for a professional convention. But since taking your advice, I'm now traveling six to nine times a year!" And she rarely pays more than just the required $5.60 in taxes per flight. Not only that, she now uses her points and miles to fly overseas each year, usually in business class. I got emotional when I read the

conclusion of her letter: "Words cannot properly express just how thankful I am to you for the traveling opportunities that have opened up for me due to your advice." This has been about more than just saving money for Lorraine, it has helped expand her world, kept her better connected to her loved ones, and given her more opportunities for personal enrichment.

I also like to use my own career as an example of just how much low-cost to no-cost travel can change your life. As someone who is self-employed, award travel allows me to attend and speak at conferences and meet face-to-face with my clients, without having to consider the travel costs. I've made trips to dozens of events for work that I might not have been able to justify if I needed to pay for them out of pocket. I've made incredibly valuable connections at many of these events. Each time I attend an industry conference, I come home with new opportunities based on the people I meet in person. In fact, just being on-site at a professional conference has allowed me to spontaneously meet individuals who later become very valuable, long-term clients. For example, because it wouldn't cost me much, I once decided to attend a conference that I normally wouldn't have gone to because its subject matter was a little outside of my area of expertise, but I felt like it might be worth making the trip to see what I could learn.

While sitting in a lounge at the conference and getting some work done, another attendee seated at the table with me and struck up a conversation. When I mentioned my work as a credit card expert, his eyes lit up and he told me my skill set was exactly what his company had been looking for. He introduced me to his boss and that marked the beginning of a very valuable relationship. But had I needed to pay thousands of dollars in airfare and hotel bills, I'm not sure if I would have attended this event, missing out on an important business relationship that could only have been formed by being in the right place at the right time.

Over the last ten years, I've used free travel to take dozens of domestic trips each year, and an average of one big international trip annually. These range from quick trips to visit family, to two-week vacations to places like Europe, Africa, and South America. In total, my family and I consume tens of thousands of dollars a year in airfare and hotels, for free or at a small fraction of the cost. And thanks to learning about points and miles, other members of my family now regularly travel domestically and internationally (like my cousin, Lorraine), and are often able to fly overseas in business class. Our family stays connected now in ways that weren't possible before.

My parents are a good example of this. They bought a second home in Colorado and thanks to the award travel skills I've taught them, they now fly between their home in Atlanta and Denver almost every month to relax and reconnect with their three grandchildren here. They've told me that they probably wouldn't have bought the house in Colorado if they had to pay thousands of dollars a year in airfare to visit regularly. In fact, I like to joke that they use Southwest Airlines like a bus service, hopping on a plane whenever they feel like taking a quick trip across the country.

It used to be that this kind of "jet-setting" was only for wealthy people who could afford to spend tens of thousands of dollars a year on airfare and hotels. But with award travel, anyone can do it, including you. It can be possible even if you haven't ever considered traveling in this way before; and it can be possible even if you are on a limited income or have found travel to be too

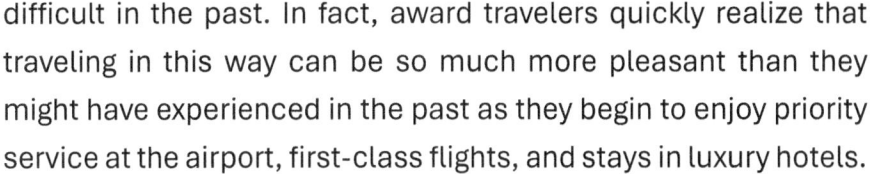

difficult in the past. In fact, award travelers quickly realize that traveling in this way can be so much more pleasant than they might have experienced in the past as they begin to enjoy priority service at the airport, first-class flights, and stays in luxury hotels.

When you learn how to travel for free using points and miles, you're not only going to save hundreds and even thousands of dollars, but you'll find yourself connected with people and places that will enrich and expand your world, dramatically changing how you look at and interact with others, and ultimately changing your life in ways you never thought possible.

Just think...

How would your life change if you could fly once or twice a month around the country to see family or to help expand your small business? What if you could take an international flight each year — in business class? Where would you go? And what if by using credit card benefits, you could skip the lines at airports and at hotel check-in counters and be upgraded to fancy suites? The fact is, you can and I'm excited to show you how.

As a professional travel and personal finance writer and an expert in award travel, I teach my clients how to maximize credit card use and spending habits to allow them to reach their travel goals. I've never failed to show them ways to realize thousands of dollars of free travel. I truly enjoy helping everyday people learn how to take advantage of points and miles so they can travel often and in style, just like any sophisticated globe-trotter or wealthy business executive.

HOW I GOT HERE

So, what brought me to this point today, where I'm qualified to share with you all the best travel reward tips and tricks?

Well, first of all, I'm no stranger to travel. Compared to most people, I've been traveling my entire life, which started early for me since I hail from Buffalo, New York — a place known for wonderful people but terrible weather! If there was ever a nice place to live that residents needed to get away from regularly, Buffalo would be it. And our family would frequently take vacations and visit relatives in warmer, sunnier places, which was pretty much anywhere else.

When I was seven years old, my family finally tired of Buffalo winters and moved to Atlanta, Georgia. Atlanta is practically built on the foundation of its airport — which would later become the busiest in the world — because let's face it, when you live in a major city in a vastly rural region, air travel becomes the only practical way to visit cities that are an entire day's drive away. Living in Atlanta forced our family to take advantage of air travel... often.

When I left home for college, I attended the University of Delaware some 700 miles by car from Atlanta, which meant I would need to fly home during school breaks to see my family, so I was boarding a plane about every other month. And after graduation, I returned to Atlanta, where I worked as a computer systems consultant, a job that required me to jump on a plane nearly every week to visit clients.

In 1997, I decided to move to Denver, mostly due to my love of mountain activities such as bicycling and snowboarding. In fact,

I had been vacationing in Colorado so often that I was getting to know people who openly wondered why I didn't just move there. But it turns out that Denver is much like Atlanta: the only major city in an even larger, more rural part of the country, where residents and businesses are almost completely dependent on air travel to connect them to the world.

Throughout all those years of airline travel my parents' advice was consistent. "Remember to always give the airline your frequent flier number when you book your ticket," and "use your airline credit card so you earn miles." It was great advice, but it only took me so far. At best, I could earn a free flight after taking a handful of paid trips or by spending an entire year charging everything to my airline credit card.

In 2002, I met my wife, Janna. She was born in the former Soviet Union, grew up in Israel, and still had plenty of family in the Tel Aviv area. After we married, we purchased two economy class tickets from Denver to Tel Aviv so that she could introduce her new husband to her friends and large family there. While we had an amazing time meeting her loved ones, the airline trip was predictably awful. We stood in long lines, sat in small seats, and endured poor service and semi-edible meals. Afterwards, we were frustrated that we had given the airline $3,000 only to be subjected to such a miserable experience. Worse, we couldn't imagine regularly paying this amount to visit her relatives, especially once we started to have our own family.

THE "AH HA!" MOMENT

Every award travel enthusiast inevitably has their "Ah ha!" moment, when the possibilities of what you can do with all your earned points and miles first starts to sink in. In fact, we can often pin-point the exact instance when we realized the astounding potential of award travel. Before that, I thought of earning points and miles as a low-priority activity, not worth devoting much time and energy to. But once that "Ah ha!" moment happens, award travelers can become extremely passionate about earning and spending their points and miles as they dream of all of the places they can go and as one of the easiest ways for them to save money on the travel they would otherwise purchase.

My turning point occurred in 2006, when Janna and I purchased an older home and began renovating it. We decided to put all of the expenses we could on a United Airlines credit card to earn the most possible miles. Around the same time, I stumbled across a United Airlines promotion that offered a large amount of bonus miles after completing a number of trips. I can't recall the exact terms, but I realized that I had just enough business trips coming up that I could complete the terms. I added up all the miles I expected to earn and realized it was more than enough to pay for our next overseas trip. And if my wife applied for a United Airlines card, the bonus miles that she received, when combined with mine, would be enough for two round-trip tickets in business class.

The plan worked, and in 2007 we took our second international trip together, this time departing Denver in Lufthansa business class, on their non-stop flight to Frankfurt. We looked around the cabin at the wealthy vacationers and business executives, and quickly concluded that we were likely the only ones seated there who took the bus to the airport. And we were positively giddy when we settled into their lie-flat seats for the nine-hour flight. We

broke out laughing when, after dinner, they wheeled a dessert cart down the aisle! Upon arrival, we spent the afternoon in downtown Frankfurt before continuing on to our destination, in shock to learn how enjoyable airline travel could be.

Following that trip, I dove into the world of points and miles and learned everything I could about travel rewards. I have always had a healthy fixation with knowledge, so my desire to become an expert in this area was no surprise to those who knew me. I had done the same thing with my job working in computers, where without having a relevant degree; I built a career in computer consulting simply by studying everything I could on the subject.

Ultimately my obsessive personality paid off, big time, as I "cracked the code" on low-cost to no-cost rewards travel, telling Janna that we'd never have to pay for travel again. In retrospect, I imagine she was probably a bit skeptical. Okay, I'm sure she thought I had gone nuts. But after our first business-class international trip, she was definitely onboard.

From there I began blogging about travel and personal finance and eventually became a freelance writer, sharing my experiences and knowledge with others all over the Internet in my spare time. I realized my true passion was reward travel writing, blogging, and coaching, so I got out of the computer consulting business in 2011 and have worked full-time as a writer and travel awards and personal financial management consultant ever since. I've written thousands of articles about credit cards and award travel for over 100 online outlets including *Forbes, USA Today, Newsweek, Time,* and of course, The Points Guy. In addition to writing and consulting, I also started producing CardCon in 2017, an annual conference that brings together the media that covers credit cards and the industry. Along the way, I became one of the country's leading experts on credit cards and award travel, where I'm widely quoted in the mainstream media and have been a guest on numerous podcasts, radio programs, and television shows.

Since I discovered the true potential of points and miles and started writing about it 16 years ago, it's been an amazing trip. Previously, few of the people I met had any real interest in learning about my career in computers. But once people find that I'm a writer with expertise in traveling for free, they just light up with excitement. The most common question I'm asked is, "How can I learn that?" This book is what I hope will be the best answer to that question.

If you're ready to discover the world of travel rewards and all its benefits, I urge you to read on. Within the pages of this book, I want to show you just how exciting, rewarding, and possible it is to travel using points and miles.

THE BENEFITS OF AWARD TRAVEL

Traveling at little to no cost can benefit you in the following ways:

Enriches your life. The U.S. State Department recently reported the sad fact that only 44.5 percent of Americans have a passport, which means that many people are missing the opportunity to improve their life by exploring the world. As I noted earlier in this chapter, when you travel frequently you are exposed to new experiences, new people, and new cultures in a way that can never be duplicated online or through movies and television. Traveling to those people and being with them helps us empathize with them in a way that we don't or can't without a physical connection.

I've always been inspired by Mark Twain, who said, "Travel is fatal to prejudice, bigotry, and narrow-mindedness, and many of our people need it sorely on these accounts." There's something about visiting a place that will forever connect you with the land and its people. I'm fortunate enough to have visited some small fraction of the world, and Janna and I have been grateful for the opportunity to introduce our three children to numerous places in North America, South America, Europe, the Middle East, and Africa. Together, our family has toured townships in Cape Town, South Africa and learned of the history of Apartheid. We've visited farms in Italy, where some of the world's best food comes from. We've stood at the summit of dormant volcanoes in Hawaii, and visited the Dead Sea in Israel, the lowest point on the surface of the Earth. For our children, these places are no longer merely just subjects to be studied in a geography or history class, they're part of their experiences and memories that they will carry for a lifetime.

Changes the way you budget your money. According to a 2024 study by Forbes Advisor, nearly half of those surveyed report that they will spend a minimum of $4,000 on travel throughout the year. When you travel regularly, it can eat up a large part of your budget. Taking a vacation or two a year, visiting family over the holidays or saving up for an international vacation can cost the average American a large portion of their income. If you travel regularly, yet don't have the desire to travel any more than you currently do, learning about award travel could be one of the easiest ways to save money. The money that you save on airfare and hotels could be used to enrich your life or your travels or can be saved for your future.

Creates closer connections. When travel comes at such a heavy financial burden and must be carefully rationed, it's no wonder that people are extremely cautious about visiting all but their closest relatives. How much closer could you be to your family if you only paid a fraction of these prices to visit them?

Flexible, affordable travel allows you to be so much more engaged with those you care about; you form bonds with family and friends across the country and around the world that can only be made through face-to-face interactions. My wife and I have helped our children develop real relationships with their friends and family members who live throughout the United States and around the world. We've all benefited from these incredible opportunities.

IS AWARD TRAVEL A SCAM?

Right about now, you may be wondering if this way of travel is somehow a scam or illegal in some way. Once you learn more about award travel, it's common to ask yourself, "Who is losing money" and "How is this sustainable?"

And that's where I step in.

The idea that award travel, or what some call "travel hacking," is some kind of a scam, and that traveling for free with points and miles isn't moral because it must involve something dishonest or illegal, is patently false. Rest assured, I would never participate in anything that was dishonest, unethical, or illegal (and I'd certainly never author a book encouraging others to participate in such an activity).

After years of studying award travel and speaking with top award travel enthusiasts and industry leaders, I can assure you

that award travel is a win-win opportunity for everyone involved in it. In Chapter 1 I will explain in greater detail how the system works and how flights you redeem and hotel rooms you book using points are by design, set up by airlines, credit card companies, and hotel chains for expressly this purpose. I will also dispel other myths related to how this kind of travel supposedly affects your credit score and help overcome other concerning objections.

For now, I'll share this little story I often tell when concerns about travel hacking come up. Several years ago, I was hosting a panel at an industry conference with the head of a frequent flier program at a major airline and the credit card industry executive that negotiated the deal for their co-branded credit card. After the panel was over, I described to this executive how Janna and I strategically applied for this airline's credit card sand were able to earn enough points each year to travel for free. I then asked, a little reluctantly, "Are customers like us your worst nightmare?" I was almost expecting him to frown and admonish me, but I was a little surprised to hear him explain that we were, in fact, among their best customers: "You're applying for our credit cards, using them for your spending and traveling with your family. That's exactly what we want." Obviously, traveling in this way poses no problem for either the airline or credit card companies or for you. The only thing it requires is that you become familiar with how to use these programs and then use them!

HOW HARD IS IT TO LEARN HOW TO TAKE ADVANTAGE OF AWARD TRAVEL?

Learning how to travel for free isn't something that you can pick up in just a few minutes, but it can be done by devoting a few hours a month to the process. And I must admit, it can be a lot of fun! To help you understand how to take advantage of award travel as quickly and as easily as possible, I've organized the book into three parts:

Part 1: The basics of award travel. In this section, I'll help you get a handle on the way you look at credit card spending and how much this affects whether you can take advantage of rewards travel. I'll also explain the different types of travel rewards, including airline miles, hotel points, and credit card rewards.

Part 2: Important details. In the second part, I'll dive into the details of the important airline, hotel, and credit card programs used to earn and redeem points. This will help you choose the programs that best meet your needs while avoiding the ones that aren't right for you.

Part 3: Putting it all together. In the final section, I'll help you put all that I've shared with you in the first two parts of the book together and give you some "recipes" for booking your first award trips. I'll also show you how to easily manage all of your credit cards, along with your frequent flier and hotel loyalty program accounts.

While learning all the nuances of award travel does take a bit of time and effort, it's not only fun but has a huge payout as well, as I've tried to emphasize throughout this chapter. By sticking with me, you will have a wonderful opportunity to learn all the tips and tricks that can make award travel worth the time it takes to make it happen.

In fact, I often refer to award travel as the low hanging fruit of frugality. Many people spend their Sunday mornings clipping

grocery coupons from the newspaper or searching for them online in order to save relatively little money on household goods. But by spending a similar amount of time pursuing and redeeming points and miles, you can end up with thousands of dollars of free travel instead of saving a few dollars a week on groceries!

For some, this book will be completely eye-opening, spurring you to become totally immersed in the subject. You may even find yourself seeking out and absorbing all the information available. If this sounds like you, then you'll be excited to learn that there are abundant websites and online forums that are always offering the latest news on the subject of award travel. Better yet, there are numerous events where award travel enthusiasts meet to share their experiences, insights, and even a few secret techniques. I'm proud to have been featured as a speaker at many of these events such as Frequent Traveler University and the Chicago Seminars.

For others, this book will be merely a beginning, giving you an introduction to the world of award travel and helping you see all the possibilities in learning to travel this way. You may not want to delve into the subject with as much gusto as I did (perhaps you're the kind of person that would rather just go out to eat instead of make your food from scratch), and that's just fine. But it is my hope that by joining me, you will be exposed to some wonderful possibilities for better, more affordable travel, and that this will inspire you to learn more and to get help from experts when you need it.

THE BOTTOM LINE

Just remember that award travel is about more than just saving money, it's about literally opening yourself up to a world of new possibilities. When you collect and spend travel rewards, you'll be able to regularly visit family and friends that you may otherwise only interact with online or by telephone. And if you're a small business owner, you can use your points and miles to attend conferences and other events that can help you expand networking opportunities — in my experience, award travel may be the most powerful tool that you have to expand your business.

Award travel presents an amazing opportunity to virtually eliminate your travel expenses, and to start traveling as much as you want. And while it might seem too good to be true, it's actually a natural consequence of the ultra-competitive credit card and travel industries that use loyalty programs to attract and retain their most valuable customers.

In the next chapter, I will explain how using credit cards responsibly will allow you to earn incredibly valuable travel rewards while ensuring that you have excellent credit. By learning about the award travel opportunities described in the book, you and your family can travel more than you have ever dreamed, for less money than you may have thought possible.

For some, award travel will be about visiting major cities and taking guided tours. Others will use their points and miles to experience adventures in the most remote corners of the Earth. Wherever you've dreamed of going, I hope that you can use this book to help you get there.

Now let's get started!

PART 1:

Discovering the Exciting World of Award Travel

CHAPTER 1:

Understanding the Basics of Award Travel

I want to begin this chapter with a story that I hope will help you see just how wonderful award travel can be, especially when it comes to making cherished memories and celebrating important milestones.

Last year, my sister Halley came to me hoping I could help her figure out how she and her husband could visit South Africa for two weeks to celebrate their thirtieth wedding anniversary. They travel a fair amount domestically but haven't taken a big, international trip in a while. With their kids grown and out of the house they were ready for some extended vacation time and wanted to travel to a more exotic, distant location. While South Africa is a fantastic destination (one of my favorites), it takes a long time to get there from the U.S. — you can count on about 20 hours of flying, each way. And the thought of spending that much time in an economy class seat is enough to discourage many travelers.

Fortunately, I was able to create a plan for them to take advantage of award travel so they could fly from their home in Atlanta all the way to Johannesburg, in international business class. Thankfully, both my sister and brother-in-law have excellent credit and manage their credit card spending responsibly, so I knew they could take advantage of credit card points and miles to make this dream trip a reality. I had each of them sign up for a single American Express Platinum card, which offered a bonus of 120,000 points each. Then, I helped them transfer their points to miles with ANA Airlines of Japan. No, they didn't have to fly to Africa via Japan, I just had them redeem their ANA miles for two, round-trip business class flights on Ethiopian Airlines, which is a partner of ANA. In total, their tickets would have cost about $14,000 if they had paid for them in cash, but through utilizing the benefits of the card's sign-up bonuses, their cost was just a few hundred dollars in taxes and fees.

Forty hours of flying goes by very quickly when you're being served restaurant-quality meals, watching movies on large, seat-back screens, and sleeping on a lie-flat seat. Needless to say, my sister and her husband had the time of their lives on safari in South Africa and made some wonderful memories together celebrating all those years of marriage. And all of this was only possible because they took advantage of points and miles they earned through their credit cards. This story just goes to show you how easy and rewarding award travel can be.

As my sister and her husband did, you can earn thousands of dollars of award travel just by signing up for the right credit cards and redeeming your rewards in an efficient way. As I noted in the Introduction, traveling this way opens you up to so many

wonderful possibilities, so let's get started learning about all of them.

First, let's look at the basics of what award travel is and how it works.

WHAT IS AWARD TRAVEL?

You've undoubtedly heard about frequent flier miles and hotel points, and most people know that credit cards offer reward points as well. But what is award travel exactly, and how do you get from having earned a few points and miles to enjoying nearly unlimited free travel?

Award travel is when you purchase reservations primarily using what's considered an artificial currency (commonly referred to as "points" or "miles") issued by companies as part of their loyalty programs. Loyalty programs have been around for decades, the classic example of such is a sandwich joint that gives you a punch card to encourage you to frequent their shop. Texas International Airlines, a small carrier that was later merged into Continental, was the first airline to create a very basic loyalty program in 1979, also known as a frequent flier program. Another minor carrier, Western Airlines, did something similar in 1980. After that, American, Delta, United, and all the other major carriers quickly followed suit. Moreover, hotels and credit card issuers decided to jump on the band wagon as well and created their own loyalty programs. Today, such programs include frequent flier incentives offered by airlines and frequent guest programs offered by hotel chains. While credit cards offer points and miles with airline and hotel partners, they can also offer rewards in their own proprietary programs.

The goal of the company offering a loyalty program is of course to encourage sales. When travelers are offered frequent flier miles or hotel points that can be redeemed for award travel, they're more likely to choose that brand over one that offers less valuable rewards, or none at all. Credit card issuers also expect that cardholders will choose their cards and use them more often when they offer some form of travel rewards points or miles over a simple 1 or 2 percent cash back on purchases. And when it comes to marketing, the allure of a free trip turns out to be much greater than some small percentage of cash back. The most skillful award travelers are those who play the loyalty game to maximize the value of the travel they earn, while minimizing the expenses that they incur. The travel providers and credit card issuers make the rules, and it's up to you as an award traveler to find ways to benefit the most from these programs.

WHAT AWARD TRAVEL IS NOT

As I noted in the Introduction, once people begin to see the magic of award travel, they're often skeptical. Some become concerned that it hurts the companies involved, is unethical, or even illegal. But remember my conversation with the credit card executive, the one I mentioned in the Introduction? His belief that people like me were his best customers and not his worst nightmare confirms that award travel is a win-win for everyone involved.

Again, it's the credit card issuers and travel providers that are creating the programs, and they know their customers will naturally try to maximize the value they receive from earning and spending travel rewards. In fact, they are counting on it.

Nevertheless, I'd like to address in more detail some of the concerns I often get from my friends, clients, and readers when they first learn about the incredible possibilities of award travel.

IS THIS "TRAVEL HACKING"?

If you have even a casual interest in award travel, then you might have come across the term "travel hacking" and wondered if this is the same thing. In most cases, the term "travel hacking" is used to describe some kind of award travel, but not always.

I am not a fan of this term, for several reasons. First, hacking is usually a word to describe illegal activity. And to be very clear, nothing I have ever done to earn free travel has broken any laws — there is no travel opportunity that's valuable enough to consider risking criminal penalties, not to mention my belief that it's simply wrong to break the law.

Also, "travel hacking" is a widely overused and misused term that's lost nearly all meaning. Some will offer valuable advice described as hacking, while others will peddle obvious or even useless tips that are supposed to unlock free airline upgrades under the same guise. Don't believe anyone who claims that dressing in a certain way, or uttering a secret phrase will magically result in a first-class upgrade. What I'm outlining in this book can best be described as award travel, and I would consider myself an award travel enthusiast and an expert on the subject. I'll leave "hacking" to the criminals.

IS AWARD TRAVEL A SCAM?

This notion is along the same lines as travel hacking, where people become concerned that traveling for free with points and miles isn't ethical because it must involve "putting something over" on someone: "Aren't you taking advantage of the airline, hotel, and credit card companies?" I often hear people ask. They find themselves wondering, "Who is losing money" and "how is this sustainable?"

Again, I would never participate in a hobby that was dishonest, unethical, or illegal (and I'd certainly never write a book encouraging others to participate in such an activity). In my years of studying award travel and speaking with top award travel enthusiasts and industry leaders, I can assure you that award travel helps everyone involved, from you and me, to the travel industry, to credit card companies.

Keep in mind that the flights for which you redeem your miles, and the hotel rooms for which you redeem your points are by design, those that would have probably gone unsold. For the travel providers, having someone occupy these otherwise empty airplane seats or hotel rooms has very little direct cost. If you book an airline seat with your frequent flier miles, the airline incurs the slight cost of additional fuel, and perhaps some food and beverage expenses, but the vast majority of the costs associated with operating the aircraft will be incurred whether an individual seat is occupied or not. And with a hotel room, there's some incremental expense the hotel incurs for a housekeeper to clean the room if you stay in it, but the hotel must still be operated whether you occupy one of its rooms or not.

The real loss the airline or hotel incurs is the opportunity cost of not selling the hotel room or airline seat. Certainly, if you book the seat or room with your miles, and the flight or hotel ends up being totally booked that night, then the airline or hotel

potentially could have earned additional revenue. However, airlines and hotels devote lots of resources to the practice of revenue management, which helps them determine how much to charge for each room and for every seat on each flight. An airline's revenue management department also tries to release award seats on flights that it thinks won't go out full, or will sell for bargain prices, so they suffer very little opportunity cost.

Furthermore, frequent flier and hotel rewards programs have been around for over 40 years, and they are consistently found to be very profitable. They are called loyalty programs because they encourage customers to return and spend more money. For the travel providers, they are essentially a form of marketing. So even if the loyalty program itself loses money here or there, it may still be profitable overall if it boosts the brand and increases its profits. And if award travelers were ripping off the travel industry, such programs would have been ended years ago. As I like to point out, it's their game. They created it, and they make the rules. When you get a great deal you are merely playing by their rules.

As for credit card rewards, it's much easier to explain why this system is profitable and sustainable. Credit card payment networks charge merchants a fee as a percentage of every transaction. These fees — typically 2 to 3 percent of each purchase — generate tremendous revenue for credit card issuers. And when you combine the revenue from merchant fees with their income from interest charges, annual fees, late fees, and other fees, you end up with a very profitable industry. But you don't have to go over their books, or even take my word for it. Just try to think of a single major credit card issuer in the United States that's ever gone out of business. I've never heard of it happening.

DOESN'T USING CREDIT CARDS TO EARN TRAVEL AWARDS HURT MY CREDIT SCORE?

This is another objection to the idea of award travel that I regularly come across... the notion that using credit cards to earn frequent flier miles will wind up hurting your credit. This simply isn't true, and my experiences prove it.

My wife and I both hold about 20 open credit card accounts. We avoid interest by paying our balances in full, and we always pay our bills on time. Our credit has always been excellent. We are regularly approved for new credit cards and we have always received the most competitive interest rates on our home mortgages and refinances.

As an expert in consumer credit, I could offer you explanations that bore you to death with the details of credit-scoring algorithms and the nuances of debt to credit ratios. But there's no need for that. I once asked John Ulzheimer, one of the nation's top consumer credit experts, if he agreed with the following observation of mine: "If someone pays their bills on time and has very little or no debt, it's impossible not to have excellent credit." He thought about that statement for a few moments and concluded that this was correct for anyone who has an established credit history (it does take some time to earn an excellent credit score if you are new to credit, so award travel may not be in your near future if this is the case for you, but working towards that higher score has its benefits, including free travel, that are well worth the effort to build it up).

The point is that the two biggest factors in your credit score are your payment history and your debt levels, so if you make your

payments on time and don't carry credit card debt, you don't have to worry about anything else. Do those two things and there's not much else you can do to hurt your credit significantly.

Although having multiple credit cards that you use frequently does nothing to negatively affect your credit score, I must be very clear, again, that to earn rewards is a strategy that only makes sense if you *consistently avoid interest charges by paying your entire statement balance on time every month*. This is such an important qualification that I have devoted the following section to understanding responsible personal financial management, and how you must have your spending and debt under control if you want to play the travel awards game.

READ THIS BEFORE YOU USE CREDIT CARDS FOR AWARD TRAVEL

Credit cards are powerful financial tools, and you should never have more cards than you're able to manage responsibly. Responsible credit card use means always making your payments on time and carrying very little or preferably no balances.

According to a 2023 Bankrate.com survey, about half of all American credit card users pay their balances on time and in full, while the other half carry a balance all or part of the year. If you fit into the latter category, it's time to consider making some changes, not only so you can enjoy a more secure financial future, but so that you can take advantage of credit cards to earn free travel.

In my coaching sessions, I often begin the process of teaching how to take advantage of award travel by assessing how well my client can manage their personal finances, and more importantly how consistent they are in paying their credit card balance on time. As noted earlier, using credit cards to earn rewards is a strategy *that only makes sense for those who consistently avoid interest charges by paying their entire statement balance on time.*

ASSESS YOURSELF

To help you see just how well you handle spending and credit card debt, I invite you to respond to the following questions. Take a moment to rate yourself to see where your strengths lie and what areas you might struggle with a bit. This assessment will help you...

- Determine if you are in control of your personal finances;
- How much of an aptitude and desire you have for learning about award travel; and
- Whether you are ready to take advantage of points and miles programs based on how well you manage your credit card usage.

1. How often do you avoid interest on your credit cards by paying the balances in full and on time?
   a. Every month
   b. 4 or 5 times a year
   c. Sometimes
   d. Never

2. Can you earn credit card rewards without being tempted to over-spend or incur debt?
   a. Always
   b. Sometimes
   c. Never

3. How many credit card accounts are you able to manage while paying your bills on time and avoiding debt?
   a. 1-5
   b. 6-10
   c. 20 or more
4. Will having multiple credit cards encourage you to spend more money?
5. Are you willing and able to put in some extra time and effort each month to manage your credit, as a price for earning award travel?

How did you do? If you can see from the assessment that you're ready to manage multiple credit cards responsibly, I want to encourage you to study carefully everything I have included in the book and fully immerse yourself in the tips, tricks, information, and how-to's I will share in each chapter. I also recommend getting familiar with the following websites to help prepare you for the exciting world of award travel:

- **ThePointsGuy.com:** This is the probably the most popular website for learning about award travel, and it's a great place for beginners to start.
- **BoardingArea.com:** This is a collection of award travel blogs from the U.S. and other countries. My favorites include "View from the Wing," "One Mile at a Time," "Live and Let's Fly," "Miles to Memories," and the "Frequent Miler."
- **FlyerTalk.com:** This is an online travel forum where users provide content, including travel reviews, tips and tricks, and help solving problems.

Now, if, on the other hand, you've found that you aren't really in control of your spending and that's why you haven't been paying off your credit cards in full and can't answer some of these questions very positively, you may not want to dive into using credit cards to earn award travel just yet. However, I don't want to discourage you from learning what you can now, so that you can travel for next to nothing in the future. Begin by working to better manage your credit card use and on paying off your balances in full every month. The premise of this book is largely to use credit cards to earn travel rewards, but if you can't get a credit card, or don't feel comfortable using credit cards, you can still earn travel rewards through maximizing paid travel and promotions, as I'll go into detail later. And I'll also cover the ways to make the most of the points and miles that you may already have. If you do have credit cards but need incentive to manage them more responsibly so you can take advantage of award travel through them, here's a little simple math on the way credit card interest works:

According to Federal Reserve Bank, as of May 2024 the average interest rates for credit card accounts that were assessed interest was 23 percent. So, what kind of an impact does carrying a balance have on you with those kinds of interest rates? Let's suppose you keep just $3,000 in credit card balances — at a rate of 22 percent, then you will incur $660 in interest charges each year. Unless you pay your card balance in full each month, you'll be assessed interest on your average daily balance, and once that interest is figured in, every trip to the gas station, grocery store, or restaurant ultimately ends up costing you far more than the original purchase price. And these costs will continue to accrue interest every day, week after week, and year after year until you

pay your balance in full. So, it can't be stressed enough how important it is to responsibly manage the way you use and pay off your credit cards. If you don't have control of your spending and debt, then there's no point in trying to earn travel rewards with your credit cards.

IN CONCLUSION...

Airlines, hotels and credit card companies have created loyalty programs as a way of marketing their services, but consumers can use them in their favor when they take advantage of award travel opportunities. When you use your credit cards responsibly, you can earn enough points and miles to take you further than you may have thought possible.

Now, I encourage you to complete the brief Chapter 1 challenge that follows before moving on to Chapter 2, where I will outline the best strategies for earning award travel.

CHAPTER 1 CHALLENGE:

1. Create a list of all the credit cards you hold (and for everyone in your household).
2. Determine if you're consistently avoiding interest charges by paying your statement balances in full or are carrying a balance sometimes.

CHAPTER 2:

Creating a Strategy for Earning Free Travel

've always enjoyed consulting with individual travelers to help them develop a strategy for earning, and spending travel rewards. One of my clients, who prefers that I refer to him as Joe Z., lives in New York and has been dreaming of visiting the Bahamas with his wife, which is an expensive vacation. I showed him how he could use credit cards like the Chase Sapphire Reserve, Chase Freedom Unlimited, and even the Chase Ink Business Unlimited to earn a tremendous amount of their Ultimate Rewards points.

When I followed up with him and asked about the vacations he was now taking, he wrote back to say, "Probably the best example is the first vacation we took after my initial consultation with you. We went to the Bahamas and got airfare and hotel, all on Ultimate Rewards points. The best part was that the Chase Ultimate Rewards website was charging around 60,000 points per night for the Grand Hyatt Baha Mar, but you showed me how to transfer my

Ultimate Rewards points to Hyatt points and get the same room for 20,000 points per night. That saved me 120,000 points!!!"

His experience not only shows how to earn plenty of points, but also how to spend points efficiently. As I always like to tell my clients, "How well you spend your points and miles is at least as important as how well you earn them." We all seem to know someone who earns plenty of money but seems to spend it poorly. Jay avoided being like that because he had a strategy for best using his earned points and miles.

In the Introduction and Chapter 1, I took a bird's eye view of traveling using points and miles to help you get an overall feel for what it is, and is not; how much it can benefit your life; the rules for playing the game; and where you need to be in your financial life in order to play that game. Hopefully I've really piqued your interest by now and I've got you thinking something like, "Yeah, I'm liking what I'm hearing — now how can I make a plan to take advantage of these points and miles so I can start traveling for free?" In this chapter, I'll take a more detailed approach and dive deeper into creating a strategy for taking advantage of award travel, just like Jay did, so you can go wherever you need and want, at little to no cost.

CREATING A STRATEGY THAT WORKS FOR YOU

Although this chapter will cover ways that most travel enthusiasts use to earn award travel, there's no one strategy that works best for everyone. Instead, the right strategy for you will be based on a variety of factors including your spending habits, travel aspirations, and even where you live. I was once speaking with Summer Hull, a fellow award travel expert whose work I admire. Summer previ-

ously wrote the Mommy Points blog and is currently the director of travel content for the popular award travel website, ThePoints-Guy.com. I was telling Summer about how I am a big fan of the Southwest Airlines Rapid Rewards program and their Companion Pass, and how it perfectly suits me and my family. But I could tell by her expression that she didn't share my enthusiasm. I realized why when she explained that she lives on the northern side of Houston and that Southwest Airlines only flew from Houston Hobby Airport, which is on the south side of the city. If she and her family couldn't fly out of Houston's George Bush Intercontinental Airport, then flying Southwest wasn't worth the inconvenience. Likewise, I've consulted with residents of Long Island, who would almost prefer to swim to Europe than fly there out of Newark's Liberty International Airport in New Jersey. For these Long Island residents, United Airlines is almost completely irrelevant, since the vast majority of their service to the New York City metropolitan area is out of their Newark hub in New Jersey on the opposite side of New York City's vast metropolitan area.

The point is, no one strategy for taking advantage of points and miles will work for everyone, so it's important to choose the frequent flier programs, hotel loyalty clubs, and credit cards that work best for your particular situation. I'm excited to now share some steps you will need to take to strategize the best award travel plans for you and your family.

STEP 1: GET ORGANIZED

Because there are a lot of variables in awards travel that you need to be aware of, the first place you need to start to create the best strategy for your family is with organization.

Take a Closer Look at the Credit Cards You Already Have

In the last chapter, I challenged you to make a list of all your credit cards for both you, members of your household, and any small businesses you own — for the purpose of assessing how many you have and the balances, if any, you are carrying on them (remember, there can be no balances on your credit cards if you want to play the award travel game). Now that you have that list, I want to encourage you to also use it to assess what kind of loyalty programs those cards might offer.

Before we move on, however, I want to stop here to talk about small business credit cards for just a moment. Using such cards is an important and often overlooked way to earn points and miles. You might not realize it, but you are likely eligible for a small business credit card. According to a 2023 Survey from Index by Pinger, 67 percent of Americans have a small business or perform freelance work, often called a "side hustle." The same survey found another 17 percent plan to start a small business, side hustle, or begin accepting freelance work. It doesn't matter if you walk dogs, sell stuff online, or drive for a rideshare company, earning income outside of formal employment qualifies you for a small business credit card, and all of the rewards and benefits it offers. I will go into more detail about small business credit cards in Chapter 5. For now, I want you to be thinking about any of the hobbies or activities you are currently engaging in that could be turned into a small side business, not only to help you earn more income, but to help you take advantage of the points and miles you can earn by having a small business credit card.

With the list of household and any small business credit cards you carry, I now want to encourage you to use it to assess what

kind of loyalty programs those cards might offer. Perhaps you are already well aware of these programs, and if that's the case, that's a good start! But what I've found in my coaching sessions is that many of my clients aren't totally on top of exactly how each of their cards work, or worse, have forgotten what's offered on their cards and how they should be using them.

Broadly speaking, there are two types of travel rewards credit cards; those that are partnered, or co-branded with an airline or hotel, and those that aren't. For example, a Delta SkyMiles American Express card is co-branded between Delta and Amex, while the American Express Gold card is not co-branded — it's just Amex.

Your co-branded credit cards offer you points or miles with its co-branded partner, while the non co-branded cards offer you rewards extended by the card issuer itself.

Credit cards are important to award travel as they offer points and miles that don't require you to travel at all. In fact, credit cards make it so easy to earn travel rewards, compared to flying, that I like to say that the hardest way to earn frequent flier miles is to step on an airplane!

The key to some of the biggest award travel opportunities available are through flexible travel rewards credit cards that aren't linked to any individual airline or hotel. Instead, these flexible rewards programs allow you to transfer your points to miles with several different airlines or to points with multiple hotel programs.

For example, Chase offers several credit cards that allow you to earn points in their Ultimate Rewards program. Those points can then be transferred to frequent flier miles with airlines like United, Southwest, and British Airways. You can also transfer Chase Ultimate Rewards points to points with hotel programs such as the World of Hyatt. Other flexible travel rewards programs include American Express Membership Rewards, Capital One Miles, Citi ThankYou Rewards points, along with newer programs from Wells Fargo and the startup Bilt. I will cover, in detail, these various credit cards, what they offer, and how they work in Chapter 5, but for now I just want you to be aware of them and whether you might carry any of them.

Finally, look into any other cards you carry to make sure you know what they do and do not reward in terms of travel. Get familiar with each card, but don't worry too much about understanding exactly how to take advantage of everything your credit cards offer just yet. While there are a number of really good credit cards out there that have an amazing array of ways to earn travel rewards, the point here is to be aware of what kind of cards you carry. That way, you can take advantage of the ones you already have, and plan to sign up for those that will offer you even greater opportunities to travel for free after you have learned more about them in upcoming chapters.

Enroll in the Loyalty Programs of the Travel Providers You Use

The next way to get organized as part of your strategy for earning award points and miles is to be sure you have enrolled in any loyalty programs for the hotels and airlines you use. For example, before purchasing a plane ticket, take a few moments to sign-up for the airline's frequent flier program. Thankfully, you can join nearly all of these programs for free, and some will even give new appli-

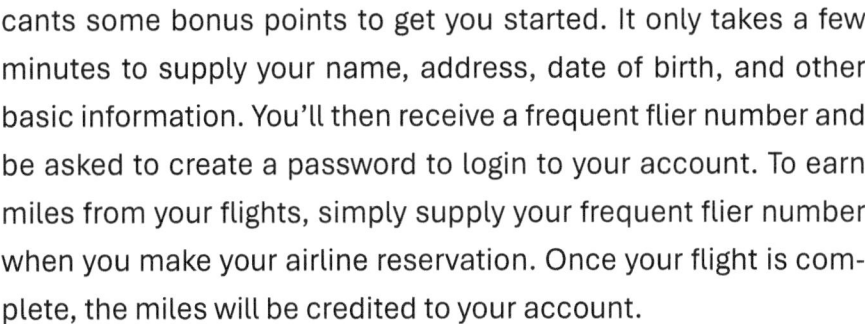

cants some bonus points to get you started. It only takes a few minutes to supply your name, address, date of birth, and other basic information. You'll then receive a frequent flier number and be asked to create a password to login to your account. To earn miles from your flights, simply supply your frequent flier number when you make your airline reservation. Once your flight is complete, the miles will be credited to your account.

Hotel loyalty programs work the exact same way. The next time you make a reservation with a hotel, simply create a free account and supply your membership number to your reservations. After your stay ends, you'll receive points. And when it comes to hotel rewards programs you have a lot of options. That's because you'll often find hotels from all of the major programs in most medium and large cities. In fact, you'll find several Hilton, Hyatt, Marriott, and International Hotel Group (IHG) properties within a few miles of each other in most major U.S. cities. In a big tourist destination like Orlando, you have dozens of choices. This allows you to select the hotel program that offers you the most value overall. Choosing a hotel program involves finding the one that offers the best value for awards, as well as one that offers you the benefits that you value most, such as suite upgrades, free breakfast, free parking, and waived resort fees. I will cover these hotel loyalty programs in greater detail in Chapter 4.

Understand How Points and Miles Are Redeemed

The final step in getting organized as part of your strategy to earn points and miles is to understand how and when rewards can be redeemed from each of your credit cards, your frequent flyer programs, and any hotel rewards accounts you may have.

First of all, be aware that depending on the frequent flyer program, the airlines will always charge additional taxes and fees for award flights, ranging from $5.60 to several hundred dollars (worst case). With hotel stays, these are taxed on a percentage of the room rate, so there is typically no cost to most stays booked with hotel points. The exceptions are hotel programs like Marriott, which may impose "resort fees" or "destination fees" on some award stays.

When it comes time to redeem your rewards, there are also plenty of partner opportunities. For instance, you'll recall that Janna and I collected United Airlines frequent flier miles for that first big award ticket overseas, yet we flew there on Lufthansa. That's because Lufthansa is a partner of United, and you can redeem your United miles for flights that are operated by any of their partners. Be sure you are aware of these partner opportunities so you understand the ins and outs of redeeming points and miles once you've earned them. Knowing this information may affect the way you set up your next travel experience, so get organized by knowing the terms, conditions, and rules of each of the loyalty programs you are involved with. I will go into greater detail about the smartest ways to redeem points and miles in Chapter 7.

STEP 2: UNDERSTAND THE FOUR MAJOR WAYS YOU CAN EARN TRAVEL REWARDS

Once you have a clearer picture of your current credit card situation, the types of loyalty programs you can take advantage of, and have a basic knowledge of how to redeem points and miles, your next step in creating a travel rewards strategy is to understand the four major ways you can earn travel rewards:

- Earning rewards through paid travel,
- Credit card sign-up bonuses,
- Optimizing credit card spending, and
- Utilizing promotional offers.

Earning Rewards through Paid Travel

The first way to earn rewards is simply by traveling with paid tickets. When you pay for an airline ticket or hotel stay, and remember to enter your loyalty program number, then you'll earn points or miles once your travel is complete. The common feature of these programs is that customers are rewarded with points or miles for making purchases from the company. Keep in mind, however, that you typically don't earn miles when you travel on a ticket paid for with points or miles. In the past, these programs worked by awarding airline passengers one frequent flier mile for every mile traveled and airline passengers could then redeem a certain number of miles for an award trip, which was free after paying taxes and required fees. Today, however, most frequent flier programs have switched to systems that reward miles based on the price of the ticket.

Paid travel is a fantastic way to earn travel rewards if you're a frequent business traveler and your reservations are being covered by your company or client. But it doesn't necessarily make a lot of sense if you have to pay for all your own airline fares. When you start earning travel rewards in other ways and begin redeeming your rewards for free flights, earning points and miles through paid travel makes much less sense and becomes unnecessary because all of your personal travel will be paid for with the points and miles you earn in other ways. But earning points and miles from paid travel will always be valuable for those whose travel costs are reimbursed by their employer or client.

When it comes to paid hotel stays, guests who participate in these loyalty programs are awarded points based on the amount of dollars spent. These frequent guest programs award several points per dollar spent, and then those points can be redeemed for free night stays.

Earning Rewards through Credit Card Signup Bonuses

The second way to earn travel rewards is through credit card sign-up bonuses. The credit card industry offers the rare combination of being both highly competitive and extremely profitable, at the same time. That's also why credit card issuers are willing to offer new customers generous amounts of points and miles, just for opening a new account and complying with minimum spending requirements.

Twenty years ago, the standard new account offer was 25,000 miles, which was then enough for a round-trip, domestic ticket in economy class. Today, offers of 70,000 to 100,000 miles are common, and flexible travel rewards cards (those not tied to a single airline or hotel program) are increasingly featuring new account bonuses of 150,000 points and more. Needless to say, a new account bonus of 150,000 points can be redeemed for a business-class international ticket or a week's hotel stay, potentially worth several thousand dollars. Earning the most generous of these new account bonuses is one of the biggest ways that my wife and I earn our points and miles.

Earning points and miles through credit card sign-up bonuses isn't just a way to fund your own vacations, it can also allow

you to give gifts to others. One story I like to share about taking advantage of large signup bonuses involves my best friend, Eric Meadows. When he informed me that he was getting married and that he and his fiancé, Charmaine, wanted to have a small destination wedding in South Africa, I decided to give them two business-class tickets as a wedding gift. Using the points from a new account I had signed up for through the American Express Business Platinum card, which was a generous 180,000 points, I was able to fly the two of them there. This bonus, along with the points received from spending the $15,000 necessary to earn the bonus, nearly equaled the 208,000 miles I needed to redeem for two, round-trip, business class tickets from Atlanta to Johannesburg (the cost at the time of this writing is 130,000 miles per person, round-trip, which is still a bargain). As I'll show later, international business class awards like this are one of the most valuable ways to redeem your travel rewards points. Going on a safari in Africa was one of Eric and Charmaine's dreams, and I was so happy that I could help make that happen.

Over the years, my wife and I have often redeemed our travel rewards for other people's flights. For instance, we've flown her friends and family members from overseas to Denver, where they've had incredible experiences such as a snowball fight on a nearby glacier or attending their first baseball game. I'll never forget trying to explain baseball to my wife's best friend, Yulia, at a Colorado Rockies game, and watching her try to sing along to "Take Me Out to the Ballgame" during the seventh inning stretch!

I cover in greater detail the importance of taking advantage of credit card sign-up bonuses in order to earn the maximum amount of award travel in Chapter 6. Be sure to check out this chapter for more information on this important strategy.

Earning Rewards by Maximizing Your Credit Card Spending

The third major way to earn points and miles is through maximizing your credit card spending. This is done by having the best credit cards available and using the right credit card for each purchase. For example, you might have an American Express Gold card, which offers four-times points (or as commonly referred to in the industry, 4x points) per dollar spent on dining and at U.S. supermarkets. By making sure you use that card at restaurants and grocery stores, a typical person might end up earning tens of thousands of additional points each year. You might have a card that you use just for travel purchases, another card for gas, and an additional card that offers the most valuable points for other purchases that don't qualify for any particular bonus. Now, this might seem complicated, but it's not as complex as it sounds, as I typically carry just two or three cards that feature the best bonuses for the vast majority of my spending.

To organize your spending to take advantage of the right card, you can use a mobile phone app designed to easily keep track of your rewards cards. Here are some apps that I highly recommend for this purpose (for a full list of award travel resources I recommend, see the Resources section at the back of the book):

- Travel Freely
- MaxRewards
- The Points Guy App

And if referring to a mobile app before each transaction isn't your thing, I recommend simply applying a piece of masking tape to the part of your card that sticks out of your wallet and labeling it with the type of purchases the card is best used for such as "gas" or "groceries." I go into more detail about the subject of maximizing credit card spending in Chapter 6.

Taking Advantage of Promotional Offers

The fourth way you can earn a surprising amount of points is by participating in promotional offers from airlines, hotels, and credit card issuers. These promotional offers can include additional rewards for referring a friend, making certain purchases, or signing up for a newsletter. For example, American Express frequently offers cardholders additional points for adding an authorized cardholder to the account, or for enabling "Pay Over Time" (a feature that allows users to carry a balance without incurring any interest charges). For example, it's not uncommon for me to receive an offer for 20,000 American Express Membership Rewards points after adding an authorized user. I'm happy to take the company up on this and add several additional family members or friends (with their permission).

Other promotions can include points for completing spending challenges. Card issuers, for instance, will frequently make offers such as 5x miles for the first $1,000 spent per quarter at grocery stores. Earning points and miles through promotional offers isn't predictable or consistent, but it's always a pleasant surprise when you come across one of them. Check out Chapter 6 for more details on this method for earning the greatest number of points and miles possible.

By maximizing all four of these tactics, you can start to form a strategy for earning all the travel rewards that you need.

STEP 3: SETUP A SIMPLE SYSTEM FOR MANAGING AWARD TRAVEL DATA

I often compare searching for award travel opportunities to looking for good grocery store deals in the Sunday newspaper and clipping those coupons. In the same way that you systematically review web sites each week for supermarket coupons or go through your locally mailed circular looking for great deals on household items, systematically and regularly reviewing award travel opportunities is a smart way to consistently save money on travel. But unlike grocery store coupons, the same time spent searching for points and miles can offer you far more savings than finding a coupon worth 50 cents off of a jar of peanut butter. In fact, having an organized system for regularly identifying travel reward opportunities can earn you tens of thousands of dollars in award travel.

This coupon-clipping analogy is an over-simplification, perhaps, of what it takes to take advantage of award travel opportunities, but there's no doubt that you can save far more money maximizing your earning and spending of travel rewards than if you spend the same amount of time searching for coupons for grocery items. While clipping coupons from the Sunday paper is a fairly time-honored and straightforward process, finding travel rewards deals is not quite as simple in the sense that the practice for searching them out is a little more involved. That means that it may take you a little longer than it would to search for great deals on food every week but is worth a bit of additional time to save thousands in airfare and hotel costs. Getting into a weekly routine

using a standard system for searching out travel rewards is the best way to make sure it happens for you.

A simple system for managing the process can ensure that you are making the most of the loyalty programs you are signed up for and prevent you from missing out on valuable promotions and opportunities. I recommend using a system similar to mine to stay on top of award travel "coupon-clipping:"

1. **Dedicate time to the process.** My system involves devoting about two hours every week to the process (or about 20 minutes a day). This doesn't mean you will need to spend this much time every week, but for me I have found that this helps me be the most thorough and ensures that I don't miss out on some important finds that may require a little more digging. And besides, I find daydreaming about travel and reading about ways to earn travel rewards to be an enjoyable distraction from my other daily tasks, so it doesn't feel like work.

2. **Peruse travel blogs.** I regularly read several travel blogs, as I mentioned earlier. For example, BoardingArea.com is a collection of many of the top travel bloggers in the world. From this collection of independently authored websites, you can filter your search to only the American travel blogs, for example, or just choose your favorites. The blogs that I have been following for over 10 years now include:

- *View from the Wing* by Gary Leff
- *One Mile at a Time* by Ben Shlappig
- *The Frequent Miler* by Greg Davis-Kean
- *Miles to Memories* by Shawn Coomer
- *Live and Let Fly* by Matthew Klint

3. **Check out travel websites.** The larger sites I review regularly include ThePointsGuy.com, where I have been contributing my own articles and content since 2012; and DansDeals.com, which is an eclectic mix of travel deals, offers for consumer products, and news and travel opportunities that appeal to orthodox Jewish communities. Another compelling online outlet I recommend is FlyerTalk.com, which is a forum that travelers have been using to interact with each other since 1998. It can take a little while to get the hang of the lingo and culture, but once you're comfortable, you'll find a wealth of information and (usually) friendly people willing to help you with your travel questions or problems.

4. **Take advantage of social media groups.** As you can imagine, award travelers love to use social media to interact and to share travel rewards information. Many are sponsored by bloggers, such as the Facebook groups for the Travel on Points website and the Frequent Miler Insiders group. Just be aware that some of the groups require a paid subscription.

5. **Attend travel events.** Another way I like to learn about the best ways to earn and spend points and miles is to attend travel events where I can meet other award travel enthusiasts in person. The events I have attended and spoken at include Frequent Traveler University, which is held several times a year online and in different cities around the U.S.; and the Chicago Seminars, which is held every October near the O'Hare Airport. There are also various local meetups that you may find in your area.

Increasingly, some bloggers are starting their own private online groups and are having their own meetups as well. These events not only allow you to attend seminars, but they give you the chance to learn from other attendees. In fact, some of the best award travel tips you can receive are often shared privately at these events, and not online.

6. **Use tracking tools.** Finally, I use a variety of tracking tools to help keep up with all the points and miles I earn each month. One of the most difficult challenges travel award enthusiasts face is keeping track of their points and miles, so I highly recommend using the following tools to make the process easier and more organized (these resources, along with others I recommend are listed at the back of the book):

   • **AwardWallet.com:** This is the easiest tool available for tracking your points and miles. It's a free website and mobile app that lets you monitor airline, hotel, and credit card loyalty programs. In fact, you can also keep an eye on loyalty programs operated by trains, casinos, and parking programs, among others. This system securely stores your usernames and passwords and can automatically log you into a reward program with just one click, acting as an effective password manager.

   • **Travel Freely:** For those who want some more advanced credit card management tools, I recommend this app. Created by Zac Hood, a friend of mine and former school teacher who lives near me in Denver, it's a pretty simple app that keeps track of the cards you have, the rewards offered on those cards, and the annual fees charged.

- Other competing apps to those mentioned above include MaxRewards and The Points Guy App.

7. **Take action immediately.** If you read about a great deal or find an offer you just can't refuse, be sure to take action immediately, if you can, while it's still available. Don't assume that you will always be able to go back later and still find that same offer. "But what if I can't take advantage of the offer just yet?" you may be asking. Of course, you won't be able to jump on every deal you come across, but just be sure to organize the information you have learned, whether you gained it from websites, online forums, social media groups, or at in-person events. You could bookmark a website or take notes, but you never know when a piece of award travel information will suddenly become valuable for you or someone you're helping with their award travel planning, so be sure you know how to access it again quickly.

CHAPTER 2 CASE STUDY: STRATEGIZING AWARD TRAVEL

One of my best friends is Shawn Newman. I met him nearly 25 years ago through a Big Brother program when he was just 9 years old, but we've remained close friends throughout his adult life. He was a teenager when I caught the travel bug, and it wasn't a surprise when he did too. Shawn became the first in his family to graduate from college. He has a degree in hospitality and event management and has worked as a manager at several luxury hotels, and I'm incredibly proud of him.

Over the years, I've helped him and his mother Jennifer craft strategies that have taken them on several European trips, often in business class. They value simplicity above other considerations and have utilized generous sign-up bonuses offered by American Airlines credit cards, which are issued by both Citi and Barclays.

Living in Denver, they knew that there were few options for non-stop flights to Europe at the time they were taking several European vacations (although there are more now), and they were happy to book awards that required them to change planes in Chicago or New York in order to reach destinations in France, Italy, the Czech Republic, the United Kingdom and Greece. By having a strategy for taking advantage of the best award travel options available to them, which involved getting organized, taking the time to search out the best deals, using online resources, signing up for the most generous new account bonuses, and using credit cards for their daily spending, they have been able to take some incredible trips that they might not have otherwise been able to afford.

IN SUMMARY...

To begin your award travel journey, you have to start by getting organized. You must inventory your available credit cards as well as your current balances of points and miles. Next, you need to start thinking about an award travel strategy, one that best fits your travel goals. And while this book is a great start, you'll want to identify resources that will offer you the latest information about the best new ways to earn and spend your points and miles.

In the next chapter, we'll take a look at the frequent flier programs offered by the major U.S. airlines so that you'll be better equipped to choose the programs that meet your needs. But before moving on to that chapter and Part II of the book, be sure to take the Chapter 2 challenge.

CHAPTER 2 CHALLENGE:

1. Take a look at the blogs and websites I recommended in this chapter. Find the ones that resonate with you and spend a few minutes a day reading them.

2. Check out Flyertalk.com and create an account. Find the answer to a question about award travel that you've always wondered about. Always try to search forums first before posting a message asking for the answer, as long-time participants can be rather snarky when new visitors pose questions that have been frequently asked and answered.

3. Create an AwardWallet account and enter in all of your loyalty program information.

PART 2:

Understanding Major Airline, Hotel, and Credit Card Rewards Programs

CHAPTER 3:

Choosing an Airline to Be Loyal To

grew up in Atlanta, and I still have a lot of family that live there. From a travel standpoint, Atlanta's a Delta town. Delta is headquartered there and operates the largest hub of any airline in the world. And the Delta SkyMiles frequent flier program has so many local partners in Atlanta that offer you Delta miles for doing business with them that my mother used to say, "If you breathe in Atlanta, they give you some SkyMiles for doing so."

So, you can imagine the resistance I faced when I tried to convince my parents to switch their loyalty from Delta to Southwest. Southwest was the newcomer to town when they bought upstart AirTran in 2011. Southwest started flying between Atlanta and Denver shortly after that, around the time that my mom and dad decided to buy a vacation home in the foothills just outside of Denver.

Every year, my parents would send all of their business to Delta, hoping to earn their basic level "Medallion" elite status, mostly flying between Atlanta and Denver. This elite status offered them a free checked bag and the opportunity for a rare upgrade to first class. But Delta's prices were typically higher than Southwest's, and at the time, Delta imposed change fees of $150 if my parents had to modify their reservations. Worse, Delta was constantly devaluing their SkyMiles by raising the prices of award seats and reducing their availability.

I decided it was time for an intervention! I explained to my parents that unlike Delta, Southwest has no change fees and offers two free bags for all passengers. And its Rapid Rewards program provides a fixed value per point redeemed. So, while flyers don't have the opportunity to earn exceptional value when redeeming their points, they don't have to worry about finding scarce award tickets either. "And," I told them, "if you can earn Southwest's Companion Pass, then you can add someone to your ticket for only a few dollars in taxes."

It was hard to convince them to abandon their decades-long loyalty to Delta and to get them to realize that they had a harmful addiction. But I'm proud to say that they've been "in recovery" for over 10 years now and have the Companion Pass to prove it. Although they've given up the hope of that occasional first-class seat they were always shooting for on Delta, they've saved an incredible amount of money, while gaining the flexibility they need when their schedule changes. This has made it so much easier and cost-effective to travel to their home in Colorado to be near my family and their grandkids as often as they'd like.

My parents' example illustrates how easy it is to misplace your loyalty to an airline and its frequent flier program. The Delta SkyMiles program that once served them well had gradually become less valuable to them, while Southwest's Rapid Rewards program had become much more suited to their needs. In this chapter, I'll show you the advantages and drawbacks of the frequent flier programs offered in the U.S., so that, like my parents, you can choose the one that works best for you.

As I cover each of the major U.S. airlines and their frequent flyer programs, I caution you not to skip ahead, even if you've already fallen in love with a particular program. Like my mom and dad, you may be hooked on a particular airline, thinking that any other of these programs just isn't for you. But as you'll see, there can be more to them than meets the eye and you might find a little-known benefit that completely changes your opinion. In addition, keep in mind that these programs are updated every year—typically in the fall—so I encourage you to visit the website for each program to get the latest data; be sure to make this a systematic part of your strategy for searching out the best award travel opportunities each year.

AMERICAN AIRLINES AADVANTAGE

As I mentioned in Chapter 1, American Airlines has a pretty strong claim to creating the first modern frequent flier program, AAdvantage. As one of the three major legacy carriers, American is one of the largest airlines in the world, and it dominates operations at its hubs at Charlotte Douglas, Dallas-Ft. Worth, Miami, Philadelphia, and Phoenix Sky Harbor airports. It also has a strong presence at New York-JFK, Los Angeles, and Washington-Reagan National.

I've never been a huge American Airlines fan, perhaps only because I've never lived in one of its hub cities. But I have found enough value in its program to have its credit cards and to earn miles in its program. And when it comes to redeeming American Airlines miles, I've received the most value when booking international business class flights on one of its many partners.

American is part of the OneWorld Alliance, which is an international group of airlines. This means you can earn miles when you fly one of its partners, and you can redeem miles for flights operated by a partner.

The OneWorld Alliance includes:

- Alaska Airlines
- British Airways
- Cathay Pacific
- Finnair
- Iberia
- Japan Airlines
- Malaysia Airlines
- Qantas
- Qatar Airways
- Royal Air Maroc
- Royal Jordanian Airlines

Other American Airlines partners include:
- Air Tahiti Nui
- Cape Air
- China Southern Airlines
- Etihad Airways
- Fiji Airways

- GOL Airlines
- Hawaiian Airlines
- IndiGo
- JetBlue
- Silver Airways

EARNING MILES ON AMERICAN

American offers travelers 5x miles for every dollar spent and up to 11x miles when you hold elite status in their program. This starts with 7x miles for Gold Status, 8x miles for Platinum, 9x miles for Platinum Pro, and 11x for Executive Platinum.

American also offers lots of miles through its credit card partners, both Citi and Barclays. And for every dollar spent on an AAdvantage co-branded card, and for every mile earned through flying, you earn a Loyalty Point. If you earn enough Loyalty Points, you'll receive elite status. Gold now requires 40,000 Loyalty Points, Platinum 75,000, Platinum Pro 125,000, and Executive Platinum 200,000. Earning elite status results in benefits such as waived baggage fees, priority service, and seat upgrades. But since you can earn these points from any combination of credit card spending and the purchase of airline tickets, it's possible to attain the top-tier of elite status without ever purchasing a ticket. This is a major benefit over other programs that require you to purchase tickets to receive status.

Unfortunately, you can't transfer points to American Airlines AAdvantage miles from any of the credit card issuers, including Amex, Capital One, Chase, and Citi. I'll discuss these transferrable rewards in greater detail in Chapter 5.

Spending AAdvantage Miles

Spending miles with American Airlines is getting harder, but it can still offer good value. The company once published an award chart that showed exactly how many miles you would need to redeem for a particular flight. But like most airlines, American has decided to make frequent flier awards "dynamic," which means it now charges varying amounts of miles for different flights, depending largely on supply and demand. Thankfully, the company still charges a fixed amount of miles for flights operated by its partners. So, while a business-class ticket from L.A. to Tokyo might cost hundreds of thousands of miles for a flight operated by American, it will usually cost much less if it's operated by one of its partners, such as Japan Airlines (JAL).For example, I once took a trip to Japan with my cousin, Noah, and was able to use a reasonable number of American Airlines miles to fly the two of us on JAL in first class, which is one step above business class. We flew from Los Angeles to Tokyo going there, and from Tokyo to San Francisco when we returned. We enjoyed amenities like airport lounge access, fresh sushi on-board, and a spacious lie-flat seat. At nearly six feet, five inches tall, my cousin definitely appreciated not having to squeeze into an economy class seat for the 12-hour flights.

As with most airlines, American's AAdvantage miles are most valuable when used for international flights in business and first class, especially when redeemed with the company's numerous partners, which will often require fewer miles than flights operated by American itself. However, you'll find that most available awards for transatlantic flights are operated by their partner, British Airways, which is notorious for imposing extremely high

fuel surcharges. These surcharges can be over $1,000 a ticket and can often exceed the price of an economy fare. These awards can make sense if you're willing to pay nearly the price of an economy ticket, plus your miles, to enjoy an opportunity to fly in business class. Thankfully, American sometimes offers domestic first-class flights for a reasonable number of miles.

AADVANTAGE STRENGTHS AND WEAKNESSES

- AAdvantage miles can be earned from several credit cards offered by both Barclays and Citi.
- American partners with a wide variety of airlines from which you can redeem rewards; business-class international awards can offer strong value.
- You can earn elite status with American by accumulating Loyalty Points with their credit cards, by flying on paid tickets, or through a combination of the two.
- By pricing awards dynamically, American often charges an unreasonable number of miles for award flights, especially overseas business-class flights, which is one of its biggest weaknesses.
- Award flights operated by British Airways are subject to very hefty fuel surcharges, which are usually at least $1,000.

WHO THIS PROGRAM WORKS BEST FOR

The AAdvantage program is great for those who regularly fly on American, perhaps because they live near an airport where it is the dominant carrier. This is also a great program for those who want to earn award travel from one of American's partners and earn miles on credit cards offered by both Barclays and Citi.

DELTA SKYMILES

As I mentioned earlier in this chapter, I grew up in Atlanta — the hometown of Delta — an airline that's nearly as much a part of that city as Coca Cola is. So, while I really want to love their Sky-Miles program, I just can't in its current form. There was a time, some years ago, when this wasn't the case. I remember after moving to Colorado and receiving my first job offer there that I wanted to fly home to surprise my parents with the good news. I simply called up Delta and asked to redeem 25,000 SkyMiles for an award ticket to Atlanta, which was great. I can also remember redeeming 50,000 SkyMiles for an economy class ticket to Europe, and springing for business class at 100,000 miles. But eventually, Delta eliminated its award charts and started dramatically increasing the number of miles it charges, especially for international business class awards. These awards now cost hundreds of thousands of miles each way.

While there were once ways to redeem a reasonable number of miles for partner awards, Delta has now eliminated those low-priced options as well. Today, it's nearly impossible to get more than about 1.1 cents in value per point redeemed. Perhaps recognizing this weakness, Delta now offers holders of their Delta SkyMiles credit cards awards for 15 percent fewer miles. This raises the value of the program slightly, but not enough to make it very competitive.

While I still like flying on Delta in certain circumstances — which dominates air traffic in Atlanta, Detroit, Minneapolis, and Salt Lake City — I caution travelers never to go out of their way to earn SkyMiles, as Delta has destroyed their value. And to add insult to injury, Delta is the only airline that I'm aware of that

confiscates all of their members' rewards when they die — all other airlines permit transferring their miles to surviving relatives.

Delta is a member of the SkyTeam alliance, which includes:

- Aerolíneas Argentinas
- Aeroméxico
- Air Europa
- Air France
- China Airlines
- China Eastern
- Czech Airlines
- Garuda Indonesia
- ITA Airways (formerly Alitalia)
- Kenya Airways
- KLM
- Korean Air
- Middle East Airlines
- Saudia
- TAROM
- Vietnam Airlines
- Virgin Atlantic
- Xiamen Air

Delta also has close partnerships with:

- LATAM
- WestJet

EARNING SKYMILES

Similar to American, Delta offers travelers five miles for every dollar spent, and up to 11x when you hold elite status in their program. This starts with 7x miles for Silver Medallion members, 8x miles for those with Gold Medallion Status, 9x miles for Platinum Medallion members, and 11x for Diamond Medallion members.

Delta offers many SkyMiles credit cards through American Express and is a transfer partner of the American Express Membership Rewards program. It also has numerous dining and shopping partners.

SPENDING SKYMILES

Delta is a fine airline to fly, and it's easy enough to earn rewards in their SkyMiles program. But when it comes time to redeem them, you will likely be shocked to discover how many miles the airline asks for. Essentially, Delta has devalued their SkyMiles so much that nearly all awards offer just one cent per mile. So if a flight costs $350, you can be pretty sure that Delta will ask for about 32,000 miles. That means that instead of paying thousands of dollars for an international flight in business class, you are being asked to pay hundreds of thousands of SkyMiles, each way. Even domestic award flights in economy will often price out at 50,000 to 100,000 miles, *each way*. It's not unusual for competing airlines to offer similar award flights for less than half of what Delta charges. In contrast, most airlines will award round-trip, domestic flights in economy class for as little as 25,000 miles, and international business class awards tend to price at 100,000 to 150,000 miles, round-trip.

Delta will occasionally hold award sales, which can make SkyMiles appear as if they have value. But these sales typically mirror the reduced prices of cash tickets being offered on sale during off-peak travel times. SkyMiles award sales for international

business class tickets are very rare, and it's been a while since I've seen one that offers significant value.

Frankly, there's not much value left in collecting SkyMiles, and the only reason to hold a Delta SkyMiles American Express card is for the benefits. These cards offer travelers perks like free checked bags and credit towards elite status, which can be quite valuable for those who travel Delta often. The airline has also started offering cardholders award flights for 15 percent fewer miles, but that amounts to just a small discount off an already inflated price. What this means is that even though I would carry a Delta SkyMiles credit card to receive valuable benefits, I would never try to use that card to earn rewards. If you want to earn free travel on Delta, you'll be far better off with a competitive cash back card that offers 2 percent returns than you would by earning one SkyMile per dollar spent. And virtually any other airline's points or miles are more valuable.

STRENGTHS AND WEAKNESSES

While the SkyMiles Medallion elite status program is valuable for frequent Delta flyers and is really easy to earn SkyMiles through its numerous travel and retail partners, as I noted previously, Delta's program pales in comparison to many of the other major airlines. For instance, Delta charges hundreds of thousands of Sky-Miles for international flights in business class; its economy class award ticket typically costs far more than Delta's competitors; and the airline continues to devalue its SkyMiles program with little or no notice to travelers.

WHO THIS PROGRAM WORKS BEST FOR

Delta SkyMiles are ideal for those who live in a city dominated by Delta, and others who fly them regularly on tickets whose cost is being reimbursed by their employer or client. But instead of collecting SkyMiles, your goal should be to reach the highest possible level of status in their Medallion program so you can enjoy perks such as waived fees and seat upgrades.

JETBLUE TRUE BLUE REWARDS

This New York City-based airline began service in 2000 and focuses on transcontinental flights, as well as those up and down the east and west U.S. coasts. Its True Blue rewards program offers a relatively fixed value for each point redeemed, and it lets you book any available seat as an award. JetBlue offers its Mint class, which features lie-flat seats on its longer flights. In fact, JetBlue now flies to Europe.

I like flying JetBlue — it offers strong service along the coasts. However, it has very few flights to most cities in-between, including my hometown of Denver, so I don't participate in their frequent flyer program. And since their points have a low fixed value, there's no exceptional value to be gained by collecting them. In contrast if you collect American or United miles, for instance, you can often receive 2 to 3 cents per mile when you redeem them for business-class, international flights. According to Benji Stawski, a fellow contributor at The Points Guy, "You can expect a fairly consistent 1.3 cents of value per TrueBlue point," which, according to Kimberly Palmer, Erin Hurd, and Sally French at NerdWallet, means you won't usually get outsized [greater than average value]: "Because JetBlue points are typically "fixed" to

the value of cash prices, it's harder to find sweet spots. ...But rest assured that you'll generally get at least 1 cent per point value at minimum."

EARNING TRUE BLUE MILES

With this program, you earn points based on the price you paid for your ticket, what fare class of ticket you bought, and if you bought it directly from JetBlue. For the fare classes called Blue, Blue Plus, Blue Extra, and Mint tickets, you will always earn at least three TrueBlue points per dollar spent. Book your flight directly through JetBlue and you'll earn an additional three points per dollar spent. Blue Basic, their basic economy fare class, earns just one point per dollar spent and you can get just one additional point per dollar when your ticket is booked directly through JetBlue. If you have JetBlue Mosaic elite status, then you'll earn another three points per dollar. The JetBlue credit cards from Barclays also offer three to six additional points per dollar spent, so a Mosaic member with the JetBlue credit card could earn as much as 12 points per dollar spent, which is a hefty rate of return.

JetBlue doesn't offer nearly as many partnerships as other airlines, so purchasing JetBlue tickets is often the best way to earn their points. However, you can now earn JetBlue points when flying on American Airlines. You can also earn JetBlue points by traveling with the following:

- Emirates (minimum 1 point per 2 miles)
- Hawaiian Airlines (minimum 0.5 points per 2 miles)
- Icelandair (many coach fares don't accrue points; for other fares, a minimum of 1 point per 2 miles flown)
- JSX (150-250 points per flight)

- Silver Airways (250 points per flight)
- Singapore Airlines (minimum 1 point per 2 miles)
- South African Airways (minimum 1 point per 2 miles)

JetBlue is also a transfer partner of American Express Membership Rewards, Chase Ultimate Rewards, and Citi ThankYou Rewards.

SPENDING TRUE BLUE MILES

As noted previously, True Blue is what is referred to as a fixed value rewards program, and you'll typically receive about 1.3 cents in value per point redeemed. You can sometimes receive a little more value when you book a vacation package through JetBlue.

STRENGTHS AND WEAKNESSES

With this program you always know what your points are worth, and you can redeem points for any available flight with seats for sale. Additionally, JetBlue's Mint class of service offers lie-flat seating that is similar in quality to other airline's international business class seating.

Weaknesses of the True Blue program include:

- No chance to earn outsized (or greater than average) value from its points since this is a fixed-value program. My goal when I collect miles with my credit cards is to redeem my rewards for the highest possible value. When miles from American or United are redeemed for business class international awards, it's often possible to receive 3 to 5 cents in value per mile redeemed. But with the JetBlue program, you'll never get more than about 1.3 to 1.5 cents per point, no matter how you redeem your rewards. This

makes the value of the JetBlue program limited, and not especially attractive.

- JetBlue's focus on transcontinental flights and routes up and down the U.S. coasts leaves the interior of the country without much service — I can't fly from Denver to the Caribbean, for example, on JetBlue without changing planes in New York or Boston, which greatly increases my travel time.

WHO THIS PROGRAM WORKS BEST FOR

This is an ideal program for those who live on or near the East or West Coast, where JetBlue offers great service. And if you are a family traveler who needs to book several award seats, it's no problem to find them since all seats are available as awards. Because there's no limit on award availability, this is also a great program for those who travel during the holidays and other peak times.

SOUTHWEST AIRLINES RAPID REWARDS

Since 1971, Southwest has steadily grown from a scrappy up-start airline to the largest carrier of passengers within the United States. Like much of how Southwest operates, its Rapid Rewards frequent flier program is beautiful in its simplicity. Points are accumulated based on spending, with different multipliers for purchasing different fare classes and having elite status.

A key feature of this program is the Companion Pass, which offers unlimited complimentary airfare for a designated companion. All you have to do is pay the required government taxes and fees, typically $5.60 each way within the United States (more when traveling to a foreign country), and you can add your designated companion to any flight you're on. Those flights include any paid with cash and points, and even those paid for by someone else, such as your company or client.

You can get a Companion Pass by earning 135,000 qualifying points within a calendar year (125,000 if you have one of Southwest's credit cards). Qualifying points come from flights, partner hotel stays, partner car rentals, and other partner activities. But you can also earn points towards a Companion Pass through credit card activity, including the sign-up bonuses for the Rapid Rewards personal and business credit cards from Chase. I'm a huge fan of Southwest, and my wife and I each have had their Companion Pass for over a decade. Later in this book, I'll explain how my family uses credit cards to earn the Companion Pass and drastically reduce the number of points it takes for us to travel.

Although I love Southwest, this airline does have a few drawbacks. For one, it doesn't offer first- class seating, and it only flies within the United States (including Hawaii), as well as Mexico, Central America, and the Caribbean. And since it has no airline partners, you can't use your Southwest Airlines Rapid Rewards points to travel beyond these destinations.

EARNING RAPID REWARDS POINTS

Purchasing tickets in its lowest fare class, called "Wanna Get Away," offers you 6x points per dollar spent. Its newer "Wanna Get Away Plus" fare class offers 8x points and its "Anytime" and "Business Select" fare classes offer travelers 10x and 12x points respectively. Having A-List status offers a 25 percent bonus on

points earned and A-List Preferred awards a strong 100 percent bonus.

Points can also be earned from partner hotel stays, partner car rentals, and other partner activities. You can earn points from the Rapid Rewards personal and business credit cards from Chase. You can also transfer your Chase Ultimate Rewards points (earned from Credit cards like the Chase Sapphire Preferred and Sapphire Reserve) to Southwest Airlines' Rapid Rewards points.

SPENDING RAPID REWARD POINTS

Spending your Southwest frequent flyer points is extremely easy. Points are worth about 1.4 cents each toward any ticket being sold, in any fare class. So, if you are traveling with a group of five, 10, or 20, then you can book tickets with your points just as easily as you would with cash. In fact, Southwest's website lets you toggle between the cash and points prices for its tickets. In contrast, it's extremely rare to find more than a few award tickets available on the same flight, for low mileage costs, when redeeming rewards with airlines like American and United.

STRENGTHS
- Book as many award seats as you want.
- Points are worth a predictable value.
- Earning a Companion Pass can reduce by half the number of points you need for an award flight.

WEAKNESSES
- Because points are worth a fixed amount, you'll never receive outsized value, which is to say that you'll never

get more than about 1.3 to 1.4 cents in value per point redeemed.

- Southwest only serves the United States (including Hawaii), Mexico, Central America, and the Caribbean, and it doesn't have any partners that serve other destinations.
- Southwest doesn't fly into several major airports including Dallas-Fort Worth, New York-JFK, Newark, and Houston's George Bush Intercontinental Airport (which is why travel expert, Summer Hull, told me she dislikes flying Southwest because its flights are too far away from her home).

WHO THIS PROGRAM WORKS BEST FOR

Rapid Rewards is a great program for those who prefer simplicity and don't want to delve into the complexities of traditional frequent flier programs. It also works well for families that need multiple award seats, and for anyone who must travel at specific times rather than just when the airlines feel like making low-priced award seats available.

This is also a great program for those who live near an airport served by Southwest, including Chicago-Midway, Baltimore-Washington International, Denver, Houston Hobby, Dallas-Love Field, Las Vegas, Salt Lake International, and others. And if you can earn a Companion Pass, then Southwest can offer value that's unmatched by other frequent flier programs, as you receive unlimited two-for-one deals on all of your airline tickets, including those purchased with points.

UNITED

I'm a pretty big fan of United, and not just because I live in Denver, where United has a hub. This airline's MileagePlus program

has been growing on me in recent years. It's not that it's really improved much, it's just that its main competitors — American and Delta — have gotten progressively worse, while United's program still retains most of its value from the good old days.

For example, United still offers a fixed price for international partner awards. Flights from the U.S. to Europe typically price at 88,000 miles each way for business-class partner awards, and sometimes 80,000 miles each way for business class awards on United flights. United never imposes fuel surcharges on your awards, which is becoming increasingly common with other frequent flier programs. I also like that United can be very flexible when there's a schedule change. When I book an award that's less than ideal, I can usually get the airline to change it to a much better itinerary if there's a minor schedule change in what I originally booked. In fact, I've found that they will often be willing to change flights to better ones, just by asking nicely.

United is also a member of the Star Alliance, which I consider to be stronger than the other two major alliances, OneWorld and SkyTeam. Members include:

- Aegean Airlines
- Air Canada
- Air China
- Air India
- Air New Zealand
- All Nippon Airways (ANA).
- Asiana Airlines
- Austrian Airlines
- Avianca
- Brussels Airlines

- Copa Airlines
- Croatia Airlines
- EgyptAir
- Ethiopian Airlines
- Eva Air
- Lot Polish Airlines
- Lufthansa
- Scandinavian Airlines
- Shenzhen Airlines
- Singapore Airlines
- South African Airways
- Swiss
- TAP Air Portugal
- Thai
- Turkish Airlines

Other United Airlines partners include:
- AerLingus
- Aeromar
- Air Dolomiti
- Airlink
- Azul
- Boutique Air
- Cape Air
- Edelweiss
- Eurowings Discover
- Hawaiian Airlines
- JSX
- Olympic Air
- Silver Airways

- Virgin Australia
- Vistara

EARNING MILEAGEPLUS MILES

United offers miles for flying much like American and Delta, with the amount of miles you receive being based on your status with their program. Non-elites earn 5x miles per dollar while Premier Silver members earn 7x. Premier Gold members earn 8x, Premier Platinum earns 9x, and Premier 1K earns 11x.

Miles can also be earned from numerous Chase MileagePlus credit cards for both personal and small business use. Interestingly, United also offers cardholders increased award access at the lowest mileage levels, beyond what's offered to everyone else. That's why I recommend my clients keep a MileagePlus credit card account open, even if it's just the no-fee Gateway card, as this will open up more awards at the lowest mileage levels. You can also transfer rewards from both Chase Ultimate Rewards and Bilt Rewards to United MileagePlus miles.

SPENDING MILES

United has a decent website that easily allows you to search award flights operated by United and its many partners. Partner award prices are reasonable but can get very expensive if you need a domestic leg. So, I often purchase a ticket from Denver to Newark, Chicago O'Hare, or Washington-Dulles in order to connect to a low-price award that's available. Amazingly, the price in miles for an economy class ticket from Denver to the east coast is often more than I pay for a business class flight overseas.

Another thing to note about United MileagePlus awards is that they can be somewhat generous when there's a schedule change. It's not uncommon for me to call United following a minor time change for one of my award flights and successfully request much better flights, so long as the alternative is operated by United itself and not one of its partners. I've even been successful asking United for better flights when there hasn't been a schedule change, but you can't count on that.

STRENGTHS

- Large global network of United and partner flights.
- No fuel surcharges.
- Flexible rules when there's a schedule change.

WEAKNESSES

- International awards often price much higher when there's a domestic flight included in the itinerary.
- Award flights on United are usually priced dynamically, which means that expensive flights often require hundreds of thousands of miles. Ironically, it's often best to redeem your United miles on flights with their partners, which are offered at a fixed price.

WHO THIS PROGRAM WORKS BEST FOR

United MileagePlus is a great program for those who want to save up for international awards, including business class. It also works very well for those who earn Chase Ultimate Rewards and use Chase's United MileagePlus cards. I especially like that I'm never asked to fork over big bucks in fuel surcharges to use my miles.

OTHER AIRLINE FREQUENT FLYER PROGRAMS

American, Delta, JetBlue, Southwest, and United are the five largest airlines in the United States, but of course, there are others. Frontier, Spirit, and Allegiant are ultralow-cost carriers that can sell tickets at a large discount. However, these airlines also impose fees for about everything imaginable. And while frequent customers of these airlines may find their rewards programs worthwhile, they don't offer much value to the rest of us, and you can't earn their miles by transferring rewards from any of the major credit card programs.

Hawaiian Airlines and Alaska Airlines both offer good programs, but it's also hard to earn their miles. Alaska, in particular, has a lot of international partners, and earning their miles can make sense for frequent customers. But Alaska isn't a transfer partner of any of the major travel rewards credit card programs. These two airlines have announced their intention to merge, but whether this will actually occur was unclear at the time of this writing.

Hawaiian is a transfer partner of American Express, and their frequent flier program can offer some significant value. In particular, using Hawaiian miles to upgrade your revenue flights can be one of the least expensive ways to fly to and from the islands in style. For example, my friend Gary Leff, who writes the blog, *View from the Wing,* once impressed me when he was able to book a Hawaiian Airlines flight from his home in Austin to Honolulu for just $200. He was then able to upgrade his flight for himself, his wife, and their daughter. As he writes, "I ultimately paid $200 and 40,000 miles each for the one-way premium cabin flight. Paid tickets were running around $2,000 in each direction." By redeeming 40,000 miles to save $1,800, he realized an outstanding 4.5 cents in value per mile redeemed.

CHAPTER 3 CASE STUDY: TO EACH HIS OWN

My friend, Nancy Olifant, is an award traveler who has an amazing knack for earning free travel. I met her at an award travel conference and over the years she's certainly taught me a few things I didn't know. But I was surprised to learn that she's a fan of Delta SkyMiles, a program that I had all but given up on.

As she puts it, "Even though Delta's SkyMiles program has gone through some negative changes for customers over the last few years, I enjoy flying Delta for a variety of reasons." She cites their onboard customer service and their partnerships with AirBnB and Starbucks. But most of all, she likes their credit cards, which offer a 15 percent redemption discount on the miles required for most flights. She even loves the LAX airport's Delta SkyClub lounge, which she finds to be an excellent place to spend time before her flights.

She holds Delta SkyMiles Silver status, their lowest level. But she explains, "Holding even the lowest status tier gives you upgrade eligibility for you and a traveling companion (even on award tickets!), and you can book Delta flights with Virgin and Flying Blue points."

Nancy's story is a great example of how a travel rewards program may not work well for some people's needs but can be ideal for others... to each his own.

IN CONCLUSION...

The major U.S. airline's frequent flier programs offer something for everyone, but it's up to you to consider your personal preferences and travel habits in order to find the best programs for your needs. In the next chapter, we'll take a closer look at the major hotel loyalty programs so that you can choose the best ones for you and your family. Before moving on to Chapter 4, I encourage you to complete the following challenge.

CHAPTER 3 CHALLENGE:

1. Which airlines offer the most service from your home airport?

2. Which other airlines offer non-stop service to your most frequent destinations? You can look up the list of airlines and the destinations served at your home airport's Wikipedia page.

3. How easy is it to earn points or miles on these airlines?

4. Which credit cards do these airlines partner with or offer?

5. Which flexible rewards programs allow you to transfer rewards to that airline's frequent flyer program?

CHAPTER 4:

Choosing a Hotel Chain to Be Loyal to

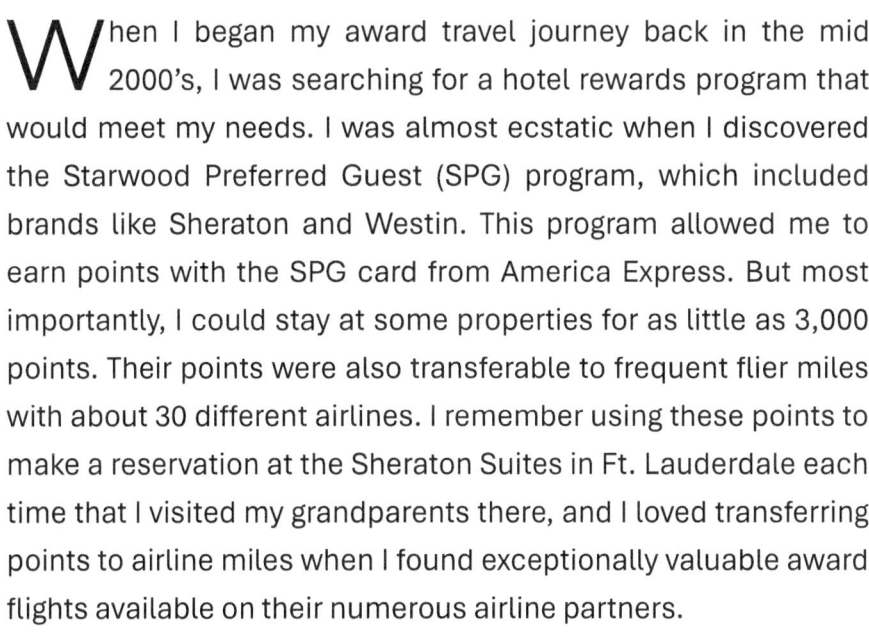

When I began my award travel journey back in the mid 2000's, I was searching for a hotel rewards program that would meet my needs. I was almost ecstatic when I discovered the Starwood Preferred Guest (SPG) program, which included brands like Sheraton and Westin. This program allowed me to earn points with the SPG card from America Express. But most importantly, I could stay at some properties for as little as 3,000 points. Their points were also transferable to frequent flier miles with about 30 different airlines. I remember using these points to make a reservation at the Sheraton Suites in Ft. Lauderdale each time that I visited my grandparents there, and I loved transferring points to airline miles when I found exceptionally valuable award flights available on their numerous airline partners.

Sadly, the SPG program was discontinued soon after it was purchased by Marriott in 2016. But there are still several major hotel loyalty programs that offer great value. In this chapter, I'll show you how to pick a hotel rewards program that best meets your needs.

EARNING AND REDEEMING HOTEL LOYALTY POINTS

While the idea of earning and using hotel loyalty programs is very similar to the frequent flier programs we covered in the last chapter, the way hotel rewards work is very different. For the most part, points from these programs are much easier to redeem than airline rewards. Unlike the way frequent flier programs have evolved over the years to the point that the value of the miles you can earn have become highly variable, hotel loyalty programs still use award charts (most of the time)so that the number of points that you need to redeem for a free night's stay will be largely predictable, regardless of demand. In addition, several of the major hotel loyalty programs offer any unsold standard room as an award, which can allow you to receive outstanding value from your points when you need to stay somewhere that's experiencing very high demand. The right hotel loyalty program will offer points that are easy to earn and deliver strong value when you redeem them. And with hotels, being able to earn elite status can be the key to enjoying room upgrades, free breakfasts, and more.

Throughout the remainder of this chapter, I will review the six major hotel rewards programs, how to redeem points from these programs, and their strengths and weaknesses.

THE WORLD OF HYATT

Spoiler alert, I'm a Hyatt super-fan so we're just going to start things off with what I think is easily the best hotel loyalty program

out there. And I'm not alone, as many of my fellow award travel enthusiasts consider it their favorite program as well.

A client of mine, Joe, is one of those fans. He recently stayed at the Grand Hyatt Baha Mar in the Bahamas and gushed over his experience staying there using points from being a member of Hyatt's loyalty program. This resort is a premium property that sits on some gorgeous acreage overlooking the ocean. From the pictures, this hotel could easily be mistaken for a luxury resort in Hawaii. Rooms there regularly sell for at least $550 per night (which doesn't include additional taxes and fees) but Joe only paid 20,000 World of Hyatt points per night and didn't have to fork over any taxes or resort fees. In doing so, he received 2.75 cents in value per point redeemed, which I've found to be fairly typical of the value you can expect to receive from this program.

Hyatt has earned their loyal fan base by offering award nights in any unsold, standard room for what's usually a reasonable number of points. Its points are easy to earn and redeem, and it waives resort fees on all award stays. Top-tier customers with Globalist status also receive free breakfast and free parking on award stays, which can be exceptionally valuable.

Here's why I love the Hyatt program: We once visited Buenos Aires and I was able to transfer some of my Chase points to Hyatt to stay at the Park Hyatt Palacio Duhau. Since I enjoyed "Globalist" status, I was upgraded to a standard suite and we enjoyed breakfast in their delightful courtyard. At every interaction, the hotel staff asked us if we experienced any problems or if there was anything that they could do to make our stay better. Although we were having a wonderful time, I admitted that we could hear some noise in our suite from the plumbing system. Embarrassed, the staff handed us the keys to a different room, which we discovered was the presidential suite. It was over 1,700-square-feet and the windows were made of six-inch thick bullet-proof glass. The bathtub seemed nearly big enough to swim laps in!

Other suite upgrades I've received at Hyatt hotels around the world have included grand pianos right in the room, and an enclosed bedroom (which is every parent's dream when vacationing with their children).Although Hyatt has been expanding its footprint by acquiring new brands, it has fewer properties than competitors like Hilton and Marriott so you might not find a hotel in every place you want to stay. But when you do, it's usually worth it.

EARNING POINTS

You can earn five points per dollar spent at Hyatt properties, with modest bonuses for having elite status. Entry level "Discoverist" elites earn 10 percent bonuses, while mid-tier "Explorist" members earn a 20 percent bonus. Bonuses for Top-tier "Globalist" members are a generous 30 percent.

Chase offers both a personal and a business credit card that's co-branded with the World of Hyatt program. Both of these cards extend bonus points for Hyatt stays, basic elite status, and credit towards higher levels in its program. You can earn Hyatt rewards by transferring your Chase Ultimate Rewards points to the World of Hyatt program at a 1 to 1 ratio, which is a great deal. Hyatt is also a transfer partner of the Bilt Rewards program.

SPENDING POINTS

Hyatt has an award chart, but the prices of the free night awards now vary somewhat depending on demand. Award nights start for

as little as 3,500 points, but you're unlikely to secure too many of those. Yet I still find that you can get a decent hotel in a mid-size city for 8,000 to 15,000 points. Hotels in major cities and fancy resorts will cost you 18,000 to 40,000 points per night. There's also a separate award chart for all-inclusive hotels, which are typically 20,000 to 30,000 points per night, based on double occupancy.

Sadly, a few Hyatt properties have now found ways to game the system and avoid offering free night awards. Since Hyatt requires that hotels (most of which are independently owned) offer awards for any unsold standard room, these outlier hotels have simply reclassified most of their rooms as non-standard in some way. The Hyatt Place Moab in Moab, Utah is one of them. Although a great property, half their rooms are considered an upgrade because they have a view of the valley. Two thirds of the remaining rooms in this three-story hotel are also considered upgraded because they are on a "high floor." As a result, you'll almost never find award nights available, except during the off season, when prices are already quite low. I've even seen the Hyatt Place in Keystone, Colorado offer rooms for cash that are less expensive than the "standard room," but still deny World of Hyatt members the opportunity to redeem their points to stay there! Other tricks I've seen at a small number of Hyatt properties include selling rooms as part of a package only or requiring a minimum stay when using award points.

These problems aren't exclusive to Hyatt, but its corporate management doesn't seem to have the desire or ability to police these rogue properties. These rebel hotels are more than happy to be associated with the Hyatt brand name but don't want to fully honor their commitment to Hyatt's loyalty program, at least in spirit, if not in writing. As long as you pay for your stay with dollars, they're happy to book you a room, but some will shut out patrons who want to pay with award points. Thankfully, the hotels that seek to game the system are still the exception, and it's easy to redeem your points for free night stays at the majority of Hyatt properties

STRENGTHS

- Strong value for points redeemed for free night stays.
- No resort fees on award stays.
- Excellent benefits for top-tier Globalist elites.
- Easy to transfer points from Chase Ultimate Rewards and Bilt Rewards

WEAKNESSES

- Some Hyatt properties (which are independently owned) game the system to prevent award stays.
- Hotels in major cities and luxury resorts can charge a very high number of points for award stays.
- There are fewer hotels in the World of Hyatt program than you'll find in competing programs such as Marriott and Hilton.

WHO THIS PROGRAM IS BEST FOR

This is a great program for those, like me, who enjoy using credit cards to earn points toward free travel, rather than those who earn their rewards from paid stays. Travelers like me are easily able to transfer their points from the Chase Ultimate Rewards or the Bilt Rewards programs for free night stays at many hotels. It's also a great program for people who visit small and medium-sized cities, where the number of points needed for free night stays is minimal. In fact, I probably stay at Hyatt Place hotels more than any other brand, as it's affordable and their properties usually offer my family rooms with two queen beds and a foldout sofa.

The World of Hyatt program is less valuable for those who need to stay in small towns, as Hyatt hotels are less likely to be found in these locations, and for other travelers who only want to redeem their points in the heart of major cities, where prices are highest.

I love this program and I go out of my way to earn and maintain their top-tier Globalist status. I retain this status by staying many nights on awards, and by using their credit cards to earn any additional night-stay credits needed. If you find that there are Hyatt hotels that work for your needs in the places that you like to visit, I strongly recommend focusing your hotel strategy on this program.

HILTON HONORS

Although Hilton offers 19 different brands that include over 7,000 properties around the world and its Hilton Honors program is very good, the program's points are worth far less than most other hotel rewards. In fact, it's kind of like visiting a country where the local currency is worth much less than the U.S. dollar. However, because Hilton Honors allows you to earn points at a faster rate than most hotel reward programs, it's largely a wash. Once you get past the large number of points required to book an award stay, you realize that there can be a lot of value in this program.

For me, Hilton Honors serves as a useful backup for World of Hyatt rewards. I've earned Hilton Honors points by hosting professional conferences at Hilton properties, and I'll redeem their points when Hilton offers a better option than Hyatt. I also really appreciate that they don't impose resort fees on award stays. If you can take advantage of its offer of a fifth night free, with four consecutive award nights, then Hilton Honors points become significantly more valuable.

I held my CardCon credit card conference in 2021, 2022, and 2023 at Hilton properties and was able to earn a wealth of points by charging my large food and beverage bills to my Hilton Honors American Express card. Later I used some of those earned points for my mother and daughter to stay at a Hampton Inn by the beach in the Cayman Islands. My wife and I then used many of the remaining points during our trip to London and Paris. Hilton offers numerous properties in major cities like these, and we enjoyed staying at the Hilton Lost Property next to St. Paul's Cathedral in London. We also received a fifth night free when we booked four consecutive award nights at the historic Hilton Paris Opera. But I've also used my points in small towns like Waycross, Georgia, where there are no Hyatt properties available.

EARNING POINTS

Hilton offers 10 base points per dollar spent at most properties, with the exception of Home2 Suites and Tru by Hilton, where you'll earn just five base points per dollar. However, those with elite status can earn 20 to 100 percent more bonus points at every Hilton property, which can be very generous.

Points can also be earned through Hilton's American Express cards, which can offer as many as 14 points per dollar spent at Hilton hotels, and at least three points per dollar spent on any other kinds of purchases you make using the card. So, like I said,

you can earn a tremendous amount of points very easily. If you are a top-tier Diamond member, you can earn as much as 20 points per dollar on your stays (excluding Home2 Suites and Tru by Hilton), plus as much as 14 points from charging it to a Hilton credit card, for a total of 34 points per dollar spent.

The Hilton Honors cards from American Express are also great for earning elite status in the Hilton Honors program. All the cards offer at least entry-level status, and some extend mid-tier or even top-tier status. You can also transfer Chase Ultimate Rewards points to Hilton Honors points at a 1 to 1 ratio, but you should never do it! It would be almost like exchanging your dollars for Mexican pesos at a 1 to 1 exchange rate. American Express Membership Rewards transfer to Hilton Honors points at a more favorable 1 to 2 ratio, but even this usually isn't a good idea, unless you're getting fantastic value from the points you redeem for your award stay.

SPENDING POINTS

Redeeming your points for free night stays is easy, and thankfully Hilton doesn't impose so-called "resort fees" on your award stays. In fact, as I mentioned earlier in this section, Hilton even offers a fifth night free when you redeem your points for four consecutive award nights. When you take advantage of this, you'll receive 25 percent more value from your points.

Hilton will make most (but not all) of its rooms available for awards at a standard price. These prices range from 20,000 to 40,000 points per night for budget properties, 40,000 to 60,000 points for mid-range hotels, and 60,000 to 120,000 points for its high-end hotels and resorts. Yet once a hotel is out of standard rooms, award stays can only be booked in premium rooms for double or triple the price. These "premium" rooms may merely offer a higher floor or a better view, which isn't worth paying double or triple the number of points. And if you have elite status by being a Hilton Honors American Express card holder, you're likely to be upgraded to one of those rooms anyway.

STRENGTHS

- Earn lots of points quickly, especially from Hilton Honors credit cards on paid stays.
- Large number of brands and properties around the world.
- Receive a fifth night free on award stays.
- Pay no resort fees on award stays.
- Elite status is easy to obtain from the Hilton Honors American Express cards.

WEAKNESSES

- Award stays cost far more points than competing programs.
- Rates for award nights go up dramatically once standard rooms are no longer available.
- Top-tier Hilton Diamond status isn't as feature-filled as top-tier Globalist status is with Hyatt.

WHO THIS PROGRAM IS BEST FOR

This is a fantastic program for business travelers whose stays are reimbursed by their company or their client. When these travelers use a Hilton Honors American Express card, they can earn lots of points very quickly.

This can also be a great program for leisure travelers who can earn points from a Hilton Honors American Express card and utilize the fifth-night-free benefit to reduce the cost of their award stays. This program favors those who like to spend five reward nights in one hotel, rather than going from place to place.

Hilton Honors makes sense for those who like the vast number of Hilton properties available to choose from, and those who want to leverage their Hilton Honors American Express card. If you can get past the inflated price of Hilton Honors awards and realize that you can also earn points at an equally fast pace, you'll see that there's plenty of value to be found in this program.

MARRIOTT BONVOY

With over 8,000 properties among its 30 brands, Marriott may have the largest hotel loyalty program, but it's hardly the most well-loved by award travel enthusiasts. I believe there are many reasons for this. As I previously mentioned, Marriott acquired the highly popular Starwood Preferred Guest (SPG) program from the now defunct Starwood Hotels and Resorts and quickly stripped it of much of what made the SPG program so special. Many people, myself included, counted the Starwood program as one of the best hotel loyalty programs out there, so it was disappointing when Marriott did not preserve the features that made it so outstanding. Later, Marriott Rewards adopted the rather clumsy name of "Bonvoy," and its critics quickly turned it into a verb. Frequent travelers who encounter problems with this program are said to have been "Bonvoyed," and some passionate critics even created the website Bovoyed.com to air people's complaints.

In addition to the loss of special features travelers once enjoyed with SPG, and the new awkward name Marriott gave the program, there are several significant problems I (and others) have with Bonvoy.

First, many of its properties impose resort fees on both paid and award stays, even for those with the highest level of elite status. Second, as with the Hilton Honors program, free-night awards are priced very high, but unlike Hilton, the Marriott credit cards aren't quite as generous in awarding points. Finally, and most importantly, the Bonvoy program seems to be getting more confusing and less rewarding as time goes by. In 2022, for example, Marriott eliminated its eight award categories and started pricing award nights dynamically. This means that there's no fixed price and the number of points you need for a free night becomes unpredictable. Whenever loyalty program pricing becomes unpredictable, a hotel usually ends up charging more points. In addition, in 2023 Marriott replaced Suite Night Awards with Nightly Upgrade Awards, which is an incredibly confusing program. I could go into more details about the nuances of this policy change and what the Nightly Upgrade Awards program looks like, but the fact that I would need to go to great lengths to do so just proves my point — it's too complex to be of much value to most travelers. These are among some of the problems that Anya Kartashova also found in her *Nerd Wallet* article, "Four Reasons to Skip Marriott Bonvoy," while also noting that their free night certificates are hard to use and that it's difficult to pool points between family members. For me, it's hard for me to fall in love with a loyalty program that's heading in the wrong direction.

EARNING POINTS

With the Marriott Bonvoy program, you earn 10 points per dollar spent at most Marriott properties, but some only offer 5x points per dollar, and you get a mere 2.5x at Marriott Executive Apartments. Marriott also offers points from its business and personal credit cards, which are offered by both Chase and American Express. Most of these cards offer 2x points per dollar spent on most purchases, and as many as 14x points for Marriott stays.

SPENDING POINTS

Points can be redeemed for free-night stays, however, there's no guarantee that Marriott properties will make unsold standard rooms available. When looking to redeem your points you may often see the price of the room in dollars along with this message: "Unfortunately, there are no redemption rates available for the dates you selected. To book with points, please change your dates or search nearby hotels." When you actually can find available awards, expect to pay 50,000 to 80,000 points per night for a mid-range hotel in a medium-size city — not much of a deal, in my opinion, when you compare that to other award programs, where a stay, for example, at a budget hotel in a smaller market will typically cost 25,000 to 50,000 points. When you consider that an award-stay at luxury properties and resorts such as the Ritz-Carlton will usually price out at well over 100,000 points per night, Marriott's point structure isn't totally outrageous, but it's not nearly as attractive as the World of Hyatt or Hilton Honors. Thankfully, Marriott, like Hilton, offers a fifth-night-free benefit, although they only give you the least expensive night.

One way you can redeem your Bonvoy points that makes the program a little more appealing is to transfer them to airline miles. One of the positive features of the old Starwood program that Marriott retained when it acquired it, thank goodness, is point transfers to 39 different frequent flier programs. Most of the time, your points transfer at a 3 to 1 ratio, meaning three Bonvoy points equals one airline mile. However, you do receive a bonus of 5,000 miles for every 60,000 Bonvoy points that you transfer. By receiving 25,000 airline miles in exchange for 60,000 Bonvoy points, you receive a more favorable transfer ratio of 2.4 to 1. And when transferring the points to United Airlines, the ratio is even better at 2 to 1.

STRENGTHS

- Marriott is the largest hotel chain in the world, with properties at most price points in most cities.
- It's easy to earn elite status through their credit cards that are issued by both Chase and Amex.
- Marriott offers a fifth night free on all award stays.
- You can transfer Marriott Bonvoy points to airline miles with 39 different frequent flier programs.

WEAKNESSES

- Marriott keeps reducing benefits and increasing award prices.
- Many Marriott Bonvoy properties don't offer their available rooms for award-night stays during periods of high demand.
- Program terms can be unnecessarily complex.
- Marriott imposes resort fees for both paid and award stays, even on its members with top-tier status.

WHO THIS PROGRAM IS BEST FOR

Despite its problems, I still meet plenty of Marriott Bonvoy loyalists. They appreciate the broad variety of properties available at nearly every price point, in almost all the places that they want to travel. This program still holds value for those who earn points through a combination of paid stays and credit card use, but it doesn't make sense for those who only want to earn credit card rewards towards free stays. This is a program for Marriott loyalists who can overlook its numerous flaws.

WYNDHAM REWARDS

I have a sweet spot for Wyndham Rewards. Of all the hotel loyalty programs I have highlighted in this chapter, Wyndham might be both the least known and the most underrated. Wyndham operates numerous budget hotel brands such as Days Inn, La Quinta, and Super 8. But when you dig a little deeper into Wyndham Rewards, you'll discover that Wyndham manages a vast number of vacation properties, also known as timeshares. These can be anything from cabins in the wood, to condos by a beach or at a ski resort and can be a wonderful way to spend your Wyndham Rewards points.

There's no reason to buy a timeshare when you consider that you can redeem your Wyndham Rewards for one of the over 35,000 vacation rental units managed by their subsidiary, Vacasa. Using your points in this way offers great value. Thanks to earning Wyndham Rewards points through their credit cards, I've had some very memorable stays in vacation rentals. My family once stayed in a fantastic two-bedroom condo beside the beach in Maui, from where we could frequently spot whales breaching off-shore. We've also stayed in a condo on Edisto Island, South Carolina, where there are virtually no hotels. And we regularly use our Wyndham points to stay slopeside at Keystone and Breckenridge ski resorts in Colorado.

Keep in mind that Wyndham now restricts awards at the 15,000-point level to one-bedroom units that are selling for $250 per night or less, including fees. Units that sell for $250 to $500 per night now cost 30,000 points per night, and those over $500 are unavailable. While this has taken much of the value from these awards, you can still receive up to 1.8 cents per point when you find a nice cabin in the woods or by the beach for just under $250 per night.

EARNING POINTS

You can earn 10 Wyndham Rewards points per dollar spent at over 9,000 hotels worldwide, as well as at Caesars Rewards and Wyndham Vacation Club properties. You can also earn 6x points per dollar spent at Wyndham properties and at gas stations using their Wyndham Rewards Earner Plus card. And if you have their Wyndham Business Earner card, you get an amazing 8x on gas and Wyndham hotel stays, and 5x on utility payments. Wyndham points can also be transferred from Capital One Miles.

SPENDING POINTS

The program is simple to use, which is another reason I like it. Wyndham hotels charge 7,500, 15,000 or 30,000 points for a free stay, which is quite reasonable, although decent rooms at 7,500 points per night are rare. Wyndham Vacation Rentals and Vacasa properties charge 15,000 points per room, per night. So, a two-night stay in a two-bedroom condo would require 60,000 points. If you hold their Business Earner card, then you get a 10 percent discount on your awards, bringing the number of points required for a vacation rental down to just 13,500 points per bedroom, per night.

Thankfully, most Wyndham properties seem to do a good job of making unsold rooms available for awards, even during times of peak demand. For example, every summer my daughter and I visit Oshkosh, Wisconsin for the massive EAA AirVenture airshow. This event draws hundreds of thousands of pilots and other aviation enthusiasts, filling up all hotels within a 60-mile radius. The La Quinta Oshkosh operated by Wyndham is not the most luxurious hotel, but it sells for $600 a night during the air show — over eight times what you might pay in the off season. But we are happy to stay there for just 13,500 points per night.

STRENGTHS

- Lots of budget accommodations available in small towns where big brands might not be.
- Great selection of quality vacation rentals at beaches, ski resorts, and other leisure destinations.
- It's very easy to earn bonus points through Wyndham credit cards.
- The program is simple to use.
- Unsold hotel rooms are usually available as awards, even during holidays and big local events.

WEAKNESSES

- Hotels are mostly budget properties, with few luxury brands.

- By doubling the price for a two-bedroom condo, vacation rental awards can get expensive quickly.
- Limited selection of hotels outside the United States.

WHO THIS PROGRAM IS BEST FOR

This is a great program for those who like to vacation at well-kept rental properties. As I noted earlier, my family loves this Wyndham option, where we can rent a condo by a beach or a ski slope and have access to a laundry machine and can cook some of our own meals. I also enjoy staying for free near large festivals and events, when hotel prices can soar.

Even though Wyndham isn't as well-known as other hotel brands, it's still worth paying attention to. If you are a traveler on a budget or want to stay in a vacation rental for free, Wyndham Rewards offers some great opportunities.

IHG ONE REWARDS

IHG stands for Intercontinental Hotels Group, and it operates over 6,000 hotels that are part of over 18 brands, including such names as Holiday Inn, Crowne Plaza, and Intercontinental Hotels and Resorts. While IHG is certainly a major hotel chain, their IHG One Rewards program is rather bush league in my opinion. Why is that? As with Hilton Honors, their points are worth comparatively less than those from other programs, such as the World of Hyatt. But unlike Hilton, IHG doesn't hand out elite status benefits quite as generously as Hyatt or Hilton. Although you can transfer points to IHG from Chase Ultimate Rewards, it doesn't ever make sense to do it. But worst of all, it prices its awards dynamically, which means that you should expect to pay a boatload of points for an

award night stay during peak travel times. So, while some people may find value in this program, I stopped participating in it many years ago.

EARNING POINTS

This program offers you 10 points per dollar spent at most properties, and five points per dollar spent at their Candlewood Suites and StayBridge Suites brands. However, you can earn an extra 20 to 100 percent bonus points depending on your elite status level in their program.

Then there are the IHG cards offered through Chase, which extend an additional 10x points at IHG properties along with a fourth-night free benefit. This allows you to earn up to 26 points per dollar spent, which is quite significant.

You can also transfer your Chase Ultimate Rewards points to IHG One Rewards at a 1 to 1 ratio. However, this would be a foolish move, as IHG points are generally worth less than a cent each, far below the 1.25 or 1.5 cents that Sapphire Preferred and Sapphire Reserve cardholders can redeem their Ultimate Rewards points for by booking travel through Chase.

SPENDING POINTS

IHG One Rewards has no award chart, so hotels will cost whatever IHG says they do. There are plenty of budget and mid-range properties in the range of 25,000 to 40,000 points. More luxurious hotels and resorts will generally cost more than 40,000 points a night. Just remember that IHG One Rewards credit card holders receive a fourth night free when they redeem points for three consecutive night stays.

The IHG One Rewards program doesn't have "blackout dates" but it does allow properties to impose capacity controls. That means that if a hotel doesn't feel like offering available rooms as free night awards, then it doesn't have to. As a result, you may find that you can't use your points at certain properties that still have standard rooms for sale, and there's nothing you can do about it. Finally, as previously mentioned, it prices awards dynamically, which is to say that it charges more points whenever the prices get high due to high demand.

STRENGTHS

- There are over 6,000 IHG properties available around the world.
- It's easy to earn rewards points through paid stays and use of their co-branded credit card.
- Credit card users receive a fourth night free after redeeming three consecutive night awards.

WEAKNESSES

- IHG charges high prices for award stays.
- Properties may impose capacity controls that restrict your ability to redeem points for free stays in available rooms.
- Their elite status program is not as generous as its competitors.

WHO THIS PROGRAM IS BEST FOR

This program makes sense for business travelers whose company or clients reimburse them for their paid stays at IHG hotels. It's also a decent program if you don't really care much about elite status perks, waived resort fees, and suite upgrades, as the IHG

One Rewards elite status program isn't as generous with those perks as other brands.

In short, this is a program for IHG cardholders who travel on business and don't really care about having the most valuable elite status.

CHOICE PRIVILEGES

Choice Hotels International represents over 7,500 hotels in 46 countries. It includes most budget brands such as Comfort Inn, Quality Inn, EconoLodge, and Clarion. The Choice Privileges program now includes Radisson America. But just because this program is mostly made up of budget hotels doesn't mean you can't find strong value in it… if you know where to look.

I like to stay at Choice properties in small towns where you'd never find a Hyatt or a Hilton. I especially like to take advantage of this program when major hotel chains aren't available or are just asking for too many points. Choice Hotels now lets you redeem points for award nights at over 300 properties that are part of the Preferred Hotels & Resorts program. These are unique, luxury properties that are pretty much the opposite of the typical Choice brand hotel, such as Comfort Inn or EconoLodge.

I've found real value redeeming my Choice points for stays at hotels in major European cities. I've stayed in Choice hotels in small towns in England, France, and Italy. Our family once stayed at the Comfort Hotel Bolivar in Rome. We redeemed our points for a room with four beds, which is a rarity in Europe. The hotel was located in a quiet courtyard that was walking distance from the Colosseum and other attractions. And to top it off, our room came with complimentary breakfast to be enjoyed on their rooftop patio with stunning views of the city!

EARNING POINTS

With the Choice Privileges program, you earn 10x points per dollar spent at their hotels. Then, there's another 10 to 60 percent bonus points you can earn based on your elite status with the program.

You can also acquire another five points per dollar spent when you charge your stay to the Choice Privileges Mastercard from Wells Fargo. Points from the American Express Membership Rewards program transfer to Choice at a 1 to 1 ratio, as does Capital One Miles. However, Citi Premier and Prestige cardholders can transfer their ThankYou points to Choice at a much more favorable 1 to 2 ratio. So, transferring 1,000 Citi ThankYou points offers you 2,000 Choice Privileges points, which can be a great deal. Citi Double Cash and Citi ThankYou Preferred cardholders can transfer their ThankYou Points to Choice Privileges at a 1 to 1.5 ratio, so 1,000 ThankYou points transfers to 1,500 Choice points, which is still pretty good.

Finally, you can buy Choice Privileges points for just over one cent each, and sometimes for less when they are having a sale. And in some cases, this can be a great deal when you are short of points and are redeeming them for a very high-value hotel stay.

SPENDING POINTS

Award nights in Choice Hotels can be had for as little as 6,000 points per night, but higher-end properties can go for 10,000 to 20,000 points per night, and more for properties in their Preferred Hotels & Resorts collection. That said, there are some outstand-

ing values when you redeem your points in places like Scandinavia, Italy, and Japan. There you can find some expensive hotels that require only 6,000 to 16,000 points for a free night's stay.

One drawback of the program is that you can only book award stays at Choice Hotels 100 nights in advance, which limits availability during the peak travel seasons or when there's a big event going on. But since many Choice hotels are often roadside stops, you'll still find plenty of award stays available 100 nights out.

STRENGTHS

- Low price of award stays, especially overseas.
- Numerous budget properties in small towns that lack other award travel options.
- Points can be transferred from Citi ThankYou rewards at a 1 to 2 ratio.
- Points can be purchased for about one cent each, and sometimes less.

WEAKNESSES

- Award stays may only be booked less than 100 days out.
- Most properties are budget brands, so there are fewer aspirational awards like you'd find at luxury resorts.

WHO THIS PROGRAM IS BEST FOR

This is a great program for those who like to visit smaller cities where they are less likely to find properties with one of the big brands. It's also an excellent program that offers tremendous award value for travelers who visit some of the countries where

Choice has a presence. And if you have the Choice Mastercard from Wells Fargo, or you earn Citi ThankYou points, then it's very easy to acquire the modest number of points needed for award stays.

This lesser-known program can offer great value to those who need to stay in out-of-the-way places, and for anyone who knows how to maximize these points in places like Europe and Japan.

CHAPTER 4 CASE STUDY: GREAT VALUE FOR WORK TRAVELERS

Eric Meadows is a cybersecurity expert, based in Atlanta, as well as my best friend for nearly 30 years. We both love to travel, but his choice of hotels is different from mine. As he describes it, "I prefer Marriott branded hotels because I overwhelmingly travel for business and value a frictionless travel experience." The key factors for him are: "Their extensive network of hotels, variety of hotel offerings, consistent quality, use of technology (mobile keys, digital receipts, etc.)." The elevated perks he receives by consolidating his stays under their loyalty program is what keeps him loyal — this despite the fact that he doesn't even find that Bonvoy points provide much value to him. "I am unable to utilize my Marriott Branded Credit card due to a company policy requiring the use of a corporate card, but I can earn points that offset the future costs of personal travel while elevating my personal experience through upgrades, early check-in/checkout, free breakfast, and other benefits that keep me magnetized to the brand," he says.

Eric's example shows how to maximize your rewards as a business traveler, as Marriott's Bonvoy program really does offer competitive rewards for paid stays. So, even though I don't see

competitive value from using their credit card to earn points towards free stays, those who travel for work, like Eric, will often find a program like this best suited to their needs.

Now that you've learned about the major hotel chains and their loyalty programs, take a moment to complete the challenge below to help you find the program that best meets your needs before going on to Chapter 5, where I will delve into all the major credit cards and the way to earn award travel through them.

CHAPTER 4 CHALLENGE:

1. Do you have a favorite hotel program right now? How does it compare to the others reviewed here?

2. Take a look at the properties offered by each program at your favorite destinations and compare how many points it takes for a free night. Then, take a look at how easy it would be to earn those points. How much would you have to spend on their credit card? Can you transfer your credit card reward points to that program?

CHAPTER 5:

Choosing the Credit Card Rewards Programs that Are Right for You

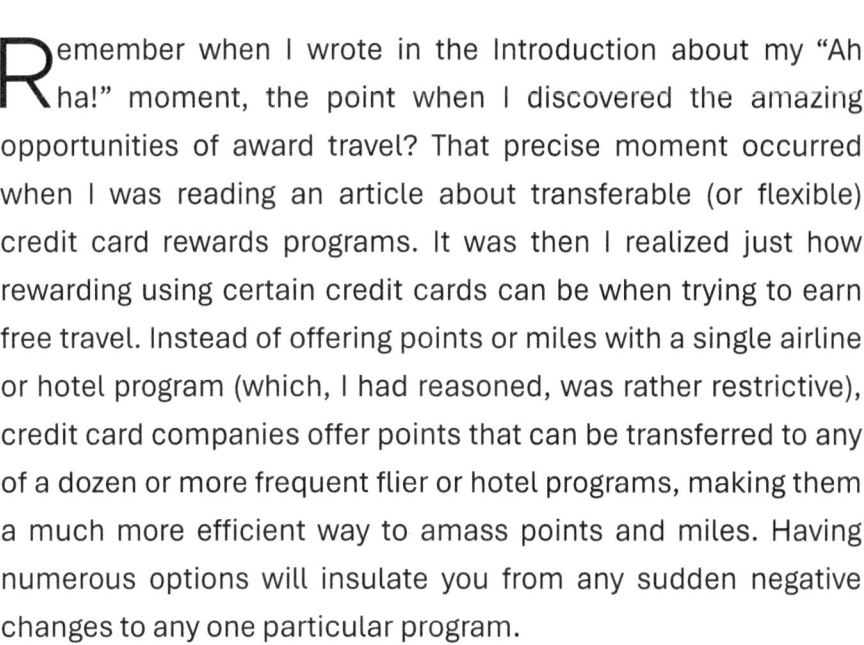

Remember when I wrote in the Introduction about my "Ah ha!" moment, the point when I discovered the amazing opportunities of award travel? That precise moment occurred when I was reading an article about transferable (or flexible) credit card rewards programs. It was then I realized just how rewarding using certain credit cards can be when trying to earn free travel. Instead of offering points or miles with a single airline or hotel program (which, I had reasoned, was rather restrictive), credit card companies offer points that can be transferred to any of a dozen or more frequent flier or hotel programs, making them a much more efficient way to amass points and miles. Having numerous options will insulate you from any sudden negative changes to any one particular program.

As I studied transferrable credit card programs, I realized I could transfer my Chase Ultimate Rewards points to 11 different airlines including United, Southwest, and British Airways. I could even transfer points to three different hotel programs: Hyatt, Marriott, and IHG. And when I discovered that most of these airline transfer partners allowed me to redeem their frequent flier miles for award flights on their partner carriers, the possibilities became mind boggling.

Let's look at United to understand just how many possibilities there are when it comes to credit card point transfers. United is a member of the Star Alliance, the international airline association that currently includes 26 carriers such as Lufthansa, Singapore, Turkish, and Air China. United also has several non-alliance partners such as the Irish carrier Aer Lingus, and the Brazilian Airline, Azul. Chase offers numerous personal and business credit cards that offer United's Ultimate Rewards points and if you transfer the points you earn from these cards to United, you could redeem a reward that includes available award flights from not just United, but also from any one of the dozens of partner carriers it has. With all the options United offers, you could book a flight from Denver to Toronto that's operated by United, for instance, continue on to Frankfurt on Air Canada, then connect to Nairobi Kenya on Lufthansa on a single ticket you book with your United miles that were transferred from your Chase Ultimate Rewards account. You could then transfer some of your Chase Ultimate Rewards points to the World of Hyatt program and book free hotel rooms!

Because you can transfer points from just one of these credit card award programs to about a dozen airlines, and you can use

miles with most of these airlines to book flights with a dozen or more partners, you can see how having points in just *one* of these credit card programs can give you access to award flights on over a hundred airlines. The moment I realized this I was ecstatic!

It's clear from these examples why credit cards are such an important way in which to earn travel rewards, so I want to encourage you to become really familiar with the information I will share in this chapter. I'll go into detail about the six major credit card issuers that offer transferable rewards points, then I'll discuss a few minor programs that also allow you to transfer your rewards to airline miles or hotel points. In each section, I'll discuss their strengths and weaknesses so that you can decide which program is right for you. Just be aware that the information in this chapter, while being current at the time of writing, includes offers that can change over time. Despite that, the overview of each program will help you get a sense of just how powerful flexible credit cards can be in earning points and miles towards free travel. To check out the most current offers with the most generous sign-up bonuses, visit my website, JasonSteele.com.

LET'S BEGIN WITH A WORD ABOUT SMALL BUSINESS CREDIT CARDS

When discussing each of these credit card programs, I'll introduce both personal and small business options. It's important as we start this chapter to mention that small business credit cards represent a fantastic way to earn additional rewards points but that this is an opportunity that many people don't take advantage of, as I noted in Chapter 2 because they don't consider themselves as someone who operates a small business.

In fact, you may be a small business owner and not even realize it. Just about any form of income that you generate outside of an employer can be considered part of a small business. This includes the tens of millions of Americans that participate in income-generating activities such as selling things on Ebay or Etsy, babysitting, dog walking, providing hair/salon services, or driving for a rideshare or meal delivery platform. And any income that you make as an independent contractor that receives an IRS 1099 form is also considered to be small business income.

Most small businesses haven't been formally incorporated. If you haven't created a corporation, such as an LLC, then you can apply for a small business card as an unincorporated sole proprietor. When you do this, you can use your Social Security Number (SSN) in place of an Employer Identification Number (EIN). Keep in mind, that even if you haven't got an established business, you can still apply for a small business credit card. Card issuers explicitly encourage new small business owners to apply for their cards before their first expense and before they start making income. When filling out a small business credit card application, just provide accurate information about your current income and your planned business income and expenses.

I remember applying for my first small business credit cards years ago, when I first started writing. I was making very little money as a freelance writer, sometimes as little as $20 for an article. But I was happy to receive the large sign-up bonuses offered by small business credit cards. It opened up a whole new category of cards that I could apply for.

Okay, let's get back to the discussion on each of the six major transferrable card programs for earning points and miles

(presented in alphabetical order, not necessarily in order of best to worst):

1. American Express Membership Rewards
2. Bilt Rewards
3. Capital One Miles
4. Chase Ultimate Rewards
5. CitiThank You Points
6. Wells Fargo Rewards

AMERICAN EXPRESS MEMBERSHIP REWARDS

American Express cards are synonymous with travel rewards, and its Membership Rewards program was one of the first to allow customers to transfer their rewards to airline and hotel partners.

If you take a peek into my credit card portfolio, you'll find lots of Amex cards. That's because I strongly value their Membership Rewards points and the ability to transfer them to a wide variety of airline and hotel partners. These cards can offer strong bonus categories and valuable perks, such as fee credits and access to the American Express Centurion lounges at airports.

AMEX TRANSFER PARTNERS

As of this writing, American Express Membership Rewards has 17 airline transfer partners:

- Aer Lingus AerClub
- Aeromexico Club Premier (part of the SkyTeam Alliance)
- Air Canada Aeroplan (part of the Star Alliance)
- Air France/KLM Flying Blue (part of the SkyTeam Alliance)
- ANA Mileage Club (part of the Star Alliance)
- Avianca LifeMiles (part of the Star Alliance)

- British Airways Executive Club (part of the OneWorld Alliance)
- Cathay Pacific Asia Miles (part of the OneWorld Alliance)
- Delta SkyMiles (part of the SkyTeam Alliance)
- Emirates Skywards
- Etihad Airways Guest Program
- Hawaiian Airlines Hawaiian Miles
- Iberia Plus (part of the OneWorld Alliance)
- JetBlue True Blue
- Qantas Frequent Flyer (part of the OneWorld Alliance)
- Singapore Airlines KrisFlyer (part of the Star Alliance)
- Virgin Atlantic Flying Club (part of the SkyTeam Alliance)

American Express also offers three hotel transfer partners:
- Choice Privileges
- Hilton Honors (transfers at a 1 to 2 ratio)
- Marriott Bonvoy

AMERICAN EXPRESS CARDS THAT OFFER MEMBERSHIP RE-WARDS POINTS

One of the things that makes the AmEx Membership Rewards program exceptionally valuable is that you can earn these points from a wide variety of American Express personal and business credit cards. All the points that you earn from these cards are automatically combined in your account. And while you can't transfer these points to other people's Membership Rewards accounts, you can transfer the points to the airline or hotel programs of any additional authorized cardholders on your account, such as a spouse or domestic partner.

Personal Credit Cards that Earn Membership Rewards Points

American Express Gold Card. This is the card I use for all of my dining and grocery spending as it offers unlimited 4x points at restaurants, plus takeout and delivery in the U.S., and 4x points on up to $25,000 spent each year at U.S. supermarkets (then 1 point per $1). Ever since it started offering 4x on groceries and dining, I've been using this card for all of my food purchases.

It also offers a $10 per month credit at select restaurants (enrollment required) and $120 of Uber Cash yearly to use for Uber Eats orders and rides in the U.S., and a $100 credit to dine at U.S. Resy restaurants. That's why, to me, this card is worth the $325 annual fee.

The Platinum Card. This card offers overflows with travel benefits including access to the Delta SkyClub, Priority Pass Select, and the super-luxurious American Express Centurion lounges. It also offers elite status with Marriott and Hilton hotels and Hertz and National car rentals. And whenever I purchase airfare for myself or someone else (or pay taxes and fees on an award ticket) directly with airlines or with American Express Travel, I earn 5x points (on up to $500,000 on these purchases per calendar year), plus on hotels booked through amextravel.com.

This card also features up to $200 a year in Uber Cash, up to $200 in airline fee credit (with one pre-selected airline), up to $100 at Saks Fifth Avenue each year, and a $100 credit towards a Global Entry or TSA PreCheck application. In fact, new cardholders could take advantage of more than $1,400 in benefits in the first year. That makes it well worth the $695 annual fee for frequent travelers.

The American Express Green Card. This is the iconic card that made American Express famous. Today, it features 3x points at restaurants and on travel and transit purchases, and 1 point per dollar spent elsewhere. It also features a $189 credit towards the CLEAR airport identity verification program that can speed you through security at select airports. This alone can be worth its $150 annual fee. For me, however, I find that the Gold card offers better value for most people.

Amex EveryDay Credit Card. This is a strong entry level card as it offers decent rewards and has no annual fee. You earn 2x points at U.S. supermarkets on up to $6,000 spent each year, and one point per dollar spent elsewhere. You also get a 20 percent points bonus within each statement period that you use your card more than 20 times, enabling you to earn 2.4x points at U.S. supermarkets and 1.2x points on other purchases. This makes it a good card for those who want to earn flexible travel rewards points without having to pay an annual fee.

Amex EveryDay Preferred Credit Card. This card is the big brother of the Amex EveryDay card, and it has an annual fee of $95. It offers 3x points at U.S. supermarkets on up to $6,000 spent each year and features unlimited 2x points on gas. You also earn 1 point per dollar spent elsewhere. This card features a 50 percent points bonus when you use it to make 30 or more transactions in a billing period. This allows you to earn as much as 4.5x points at U.S. supermarkets, 3x on gas, and 1.5x elsewhere. There's a lot of award travel experts that will use this card on all of their spending that doesn't qualify for a bonus, so that they can earn at least 1.5x on all purchases.

American Express Small Business Cards that Earn Membership Rewards Points

Business Gold Card. This is a very strong small business card that offers 4x points on your top two categories of business spending, including:

- Airfare purchased directly from airlines;
- U.S. purchases for advertising in select media (online, TV, radio);
- U.S. purchases made directly from select technology providers of computer hardware, software, and cloud solutions;
- U.S. purchases at gas stations;
- U.S. purchases at restaurants, including takeout and delivery; and
- U.S. purchases for shipping.

I've spoken with several small business owners who spend heavily in these areas, such as those with a fleet of vehicles who make large gas purchases. These cardholders are able to rake in the points on this card, making it worth the $295 annual fee.

The Business Platinum Card. Like the personal version of the Platinum Card, the small business version is full of features, and fee credits. You get access to the Delta SkyClub, Priority Pass Select, and American Express Centurion lounges. And it comes with elite status for Marriott and Hilton hotels and Hertz and National car rentals, and 5x points on prepaid airfare and hotels booked through amextravel.com. It also offers $200 in annual incidental airline fees credit with a pre-selected airline, up to $400 in statement credits for purchases with Dell annually (split into up to $200 credit semi-annually), and up to a $100 credit towards Global Entry or TSA PreCheck application fees. If you can use most of these benefits, then this card can be worth the annual fee of $695.

Business Green Rewards Card. This is a modest small business card that offers 2x points on flights and prepaid hotels booked through Amex Travel. Otherwise, it's just a simple card with a manageable $95 annual fee.

Blue Business® Plus Credit Card. This card offers 2x points on all purchases up to $50,000 spent each calendar year. This makes it a great card for earning points on purchases that aren't eligible for any other bonus. And there's no annual fee for this card.

AMERICAN EXPRESS MEMBERSHIP REWARDS STRENGTHS

This program is one of my favorites for several reasons. First, it offers a wide variety of airline and hotel partners. For me, their most valuable partners have been Air Canada, Singapore, Emirates, Al Nippon Airlines (ANA), and Qantas. Air Canada's Aeroplan is a strong program that's part of the Star Alliance, and it has many non-alliance partners. Emirates can be a good option, especially for their one-off flights from Newark to Athens and New York-JFK to Milan Malpensa.

ANA, which is a Japanese carrier, is one I've never flown, but I frequently transfer miles to its program as it offers outstanding value. For 100,000 points, you can book a round-trip, business class ticket between North America and Europe on any of ANA's Star Alliance partners. For example, with 130,000 miles you can get a round-trip, business class ticket from North America to the Middle East or Africa, which is extraordinary. However, just be aware that ANA requires the purchase of a round-trip ticket, and that it can impose hefty fuel surcharges for award flights on partners such as Lufthansa, Swiss, and Austrian. How high? How does $1,000 per person each way sound? So just be aware that you could be paying about the cost of an economy class ticket, as well as your miles, to fly in business class, so be sure you book using one of their Star Alliance partner airlines that do not charge these hefty fees.

Another fantastic transfer partner in this program is the Australian airline Qantas. It's OneWorld member but also counts El Al Israeli airlines as a partner. Redeeming Qantas miles is one of the few ways to book El Al award flights, which has value.

When it comes to hotels, Choice Privileges is a strong program that you can earn points with using the American Express Membership Rewards program, and you can transfer points to Hilton at a 1 to 2 ratio, which provides a good value. But under no circumstances would I ever transfer valuable American Express Membership Rewards points at a 1 to 1 ratio to comparatively low-value Marriott Bonvoy points (see Chapter4 for my take on the Marriott Bonvoy program).

Most importantly, American Express offers a strong lineup of both business and personal cards that earn Membership Rewards points, and it frequently features transfer bonuses that make your points even more valuable. For example, it's not uncommon for American Express to offer a 30 percent bonus when you transfer your points to one or more featured frequent flier programs.

WEAKNESSES

This program lacks three of the most important transfer partners that Chase Ultimate Rewards offers, which are United, Southwest, and Hyatt. Southwest is the largest domestic carrier in the U.S. while United has a great Star Alliance program. Hyatt is perhaps the leading hotel rewards program, but you can't transfer your Amex points there. And while Membership Rewards points can be transferred to Delta, which isn't a partner of any other of the major transferable credit card rewards program, as I've shown earlier (see Chapter3), Delta SkyMiles are worth little compared to most other frequent flier miles.

WHO THIS PROGRAM IS BEST FOR

This is a great program for people who are saving up for international award flights in business class, as its transfer partners have a lot of bases covered. And while you can't use it to top off your United, Southwest, and Hyatt accounts, having access to high-value frequent flier programs like ANA and Qantas makes the American Express Membership Rewards one of the most valuable flexible credit card rewards programs offered.

BILT REWARDS

Bilt is one of the newer flexible travel rewards programs, and one of the smallest. But it has a few distinct advantages over its competitors that make it worth considering. Specifically, Bilt Rewards is the only program that allows you to earn points on your rent payments, without paying any fees. And while there is a credit card that offers Bilt points, you can actually join the Bilt Rewards

program without being a cardholder, which is a really nice option. I've been a close observer of Bilt since it started up, and I'm convinced it's on its way to becoming a major player in the future.

I've recommended the Bilt card to many friends and family members who rent, and they are all very satisfied with it. For them, it's an easy way to earn tens of thousands of transferrable points each year from their rent payments, while taking advantage of Bilt's frequent monthly promotions that include new ways to earn and redeem points.

BILT AIRLINE PARTNERS

- Aer Lingus Aer Club
- Air Canada Aeroplan (part of the Star Alliance)
- Alaska Airlines (part of the OneWorld Alliance)
- Cathay Pacific Asia Miles (part of the OneWorld Alliance)
- British Airways Executive Club (part of the OneWorld Alliance)
- Emirates Skywards
- Air France/KLM Flying Blue (part of the OneWorld Alliance)
- Hawaiian Airlines Hawaiian Miles
- Iberia Plus (part of the OneWorld Alliance)
- Turkish Miles & Smiles (part of the Star Alliance)
- Virgin Points (part of the SkyTeam Alliance)
- United Mileage Plus (part of the Star Alliance)

HOTEL PARTNERS

- World of Hyatt
- IHG One Rewards

CREDIT CARDS THAT OFFER BILT REWARDS POINTS

As of this writing, there is only a single credit card that offers Bilt Rewards points, the Bilt Rewards Mastercard, issued by Wells Fargo. This card gives you 1 point per dollar spent on rent. When you charge your rent to your Bilt Mastercard, it will pay your landlord electronically, or issue them a check.

To earn points on rent payments, you just have to use your card to make five transactions every statement period, and there's a limit of 100,000 points per calendar year.

The Bilt Mastercard also offers 2x points on travel, 3x points on dining, and 1 point per dollar spent elsewhere. It offers numerous promotions for earning extra points for specific purchases. For example, it offers double points on the first day of the month, which it calls "Rent Day." In addition, every month there could be other offers, such as 10x on dining or transfer bonuses that could double the miles you receive when you transfer your rewards to airline miles. This card also offers numerous travel insurance and purchase protection policies, which is remarkable for a card with no annual fees.

BILT STRENGTHS

Bilt is the only program that allows you to pay rent *without any fees*. In contrast, there are other services that allow you to use a credit card to pay rent, but they charge a fee of 3 percent or more, which typically exceeds the value of the rewards you would earn. The Bilt Rewards program is the only one that offers transfers to American Airlines. It has a wide variety of valuable transfer partners including the World of Hyatt, Air Canada Aeroplan, and United.

WEAKNESSES

The program only offers a single credit card and Bilt Rewards must be transferred in increments of 2,000 points at a time. But I see the number of cards that will get on board with this program increasing over the next few years.

WHO THIS PROGRAM IS BEST FOR

I recommend Bilt for anyone who rents a home or apartment, especially young adults who are just getting started using credit cards and earning travel rewards. For renters, this is a no-brainer — you're leaving rewards on the table every month if you don't pay your rent through Bilt. Even for those who don't rent, the Bilt Rewards Mastercard represents one of the few ways to earn valuable transferable points without paying an annual fee. Furthermore, some homeowners report that they can pay HOA fees with their Bilt card, and there's talk of Bilt cardholders being able to make mortgage payments one day using the card. That said, I see participation in the Bilt Rewards program as a way to complement a deeper relationship with one or more of the other major programs that offer a variety of personal and small business credit cards.

CAPITAL ONE MILES

Capital One Miles is one of the more recent transferable travel rewards programs. This program started many years ago with the Capital One Venture card, but originally the points were only worth 1 cent each as statement credits towards travel purchases.

But in recent years, Capital One has expanded their rewards program to encompass several personal and small business credit cards, and now offers the ability to transfer their miles to airline and hotel programs.

I like Capital One as it's the youngest of all the major credit card issuers and still has more of a start-up mentality than its older competitors that were founded in the 1800s. In an industry where companies often just follow their competitors, Capital One likes to innovate.

CAPITAL ONE PARTNERS

Airlines:

- Aeromexico Club Premier (part of the SkyTeam Alliance)
- Air Canada Aeroplan (part of the Star Alliance)
- Cathay Pacific Asia Miles (part of the OneWorld Alliance)
- Avianca LifeMiles (part of the Star Alliance)
- British Airways Executive Club (part of the OneWorld Alliance)
- Emirates Skywards
- Etihad Guest
- EVA Air Infinity MileageLands (part of the Star Alliance, 2:1.5 ratio)
- Finnair Plus (part of the OneWorld Alliance)
- Air France/ KLM Flying Blue (part of the SkyTeam Alliance)
- Qantas Frequent Flyer (part of the OneWorld Alliance)
- Singapore Airlines KrisFlyer (part of the Star Alliance)
- TAP Air Portugal Miles&Go (part of the Star Alliance)
- Turkish Airlines Miles & Smiles (part of the Star Alliance)
- Virgin Red (part of the SkyTeam Alliance)

Hotels:

- Choice Privileges
- Accor Live Limitless (2 to 1 transfer ratio)
- Wyndham Rewards

PERSONAL CREDIT CARDS THAT EARN CAPITAL ONE MILES

VentureOne Rewards. This is Capital One's entry-level travel rewards card. It earns 1.25 miles per dollar spent and has no annual fee. It's typically available in a standard version with a sign-up bonus, and a version for those with good, rather than excellent credit, that doesn't offer a sign-up bonus.

Venture Rewards. This was Capital One's flagship travel rewards card, at least until the premium Venture X Rewards card appeared. This card offers 2x miles per dollar spent on all purchases with no limits. It also features a $100 credit towards a Global Entry or TSA PreCheck application. It has a $95 annual fee.

Venture X Rewards. This premium travel rewards card offers 2x miles per dollar spent on all purchases and features a $100 credit towards a Global Entry or TSA PreCheck application. It also offers 10x miles on hotels and rental cars booked through Capital One Travel and 5x miles on flights booked through Capital One Travel. It includes a Priority Pass Select airport lounge membership, and its $395 annual fee is mostly offset by a $300 annual credit towards travel booked through Capital One. The Venture X is a great card for those who are new to earning travel rewards. You can't go wrong with earning 2x on everything, and the lounge access is a great perk at this price point.

SMALL BUSINESS CREDIT CARDS THAT EARN CAPITAL ONE MILES

Spark 2x Miles. Like the Venture card, this card offers 2x miles on all purchases and features a $100 credit towards a Global Entry or TSA PreCheck application. It has a $95 annual fee, which is often waived the first year.

Spark 1.5x Miles Select. As its name implies, this version of the Capital One Spark card offers just 1.5 miles per dollar spent. What makes it attractive is that it has no annual fee.

Venture X Business. This is the small business version of the Venture X Rewards card. Just like its consumer counterpart, it offers 2x miles per dollar spent on all purchases and features a $100 credit towards a Global Entry or TSA PreCheck application. It also offers 10X miles on hotels and rental cars booked through Capital One Travel and 5x miles on flights booked through Capital One Travel. It includes a Priority Pass Select airport lounge membership, and its $395 annual fee is mostly offset by a $300 annual credit towards travel booked through

Capital One. But you must apply for this card through a Capital One small business relationship manager.

CAPITAL ONE MILES STRENGTHS

- This program has a strong list of international airline transfer partners.
- Capital One has several cards that offer 2x miles per dollar spent.
- It offers entry level and premium rewards cards for both consumers and small business owners.

- Allows transfers to Wyndham Rewards, which I'ma big fan of because it includes plenty of budget properties and also a lot of vacation rental homes managed by Vacasa.

WEAKNESSES

None of Capital One's airline transfer partners are domestic carriers, but most have domestic partners. As good as their transfer partners are, there aren't any that stand out and aren't available from other major competing programs.

WHO THIS PROGRAM IS BEST FOR

This is a great program for those who know how to get the most out of their foreign transfer partners such as Qantas and Turkish. Foreign transfer partners like these can offer some unique reward options. For example, Qantas offers rewards on El Al Israeli airlines and Turkish is known for offering award flights with United to Hawaii for 10,000 miles each way, the same as any other domestic award.

Transfers to Wyndham can be very valuable, especially when using those points for vacation rentals from Vacasa. And if you are a big spender, then you will do really well by earning double miles on your purchases, both business and personal.

CHASE ULTIMATE REWARDS

Ask me what my favorite credit card rewards program is and I'll probably answer "Chase" before you can finish your sentence. That's because I value Chase Ultimate Rewards points more than those from any other credit card rewards program.

The reason is that Chase offers some rare or unique transfer partners such as United, Hyatt, and Southwest. I also love this program because you can easily earn points from numerous small business and personal credit cards such as the wildly popular Chase Sapphire Preferred and Sapphire Reserve cards.

CHASE PARTNERS

Airlines:

- Aer Lingus Aer Club
- Air Canada Aeroplan (part of the Star Alliance)
- Air France-KLM Flying Blue (part of the SkyTeam Alliance)
- British Airways Executive Club (part of the OneWorld Alliance)
- Emirates Skywards
- Iberia Plus (part of the OneWorld Alliance)
- JetBlue TrueBlue
- Singapore Airlines KrisFlyer (part of the Star Alliance)
- Southwest Airlines Rapid Rewards
- United MileagePlus (part of the Star Alliance)
- Virgin Atlantic Flying Club (part of the SkyTeam Alliance)

Hotels:

- IHG Rewards Club Hotels
- Marriott Bonvoy
- World of Hyatt

CHASE CREDIT CARDS THAT OFFER CHASE ULTIMATE RE-WARDS POINTS

Personal Chase Credit Cards

Freedom Unlimited. Even though Chase markets this card as offering cash back, it actually offers 1.5x points per dollar spent. It also features 3x on dining and delivery, 3x at drugstores, and 5x on travel purchased through Chase. So, this is a great card to use when spending in its bonus categories or when making a purchase that doesn't otherwise offer a bonus. That's because 1.5x points is 50 percent more than the 1x that most other cards offer for non-bonus purchases. By itself, you can't transfer these points to travel partners, but you can also combine these points with your Chase Sapphire Preferred, Sapphire Reserve, or Ink Business Preferred. And best of all, there's no annual fee for this card.

Freedom Flex. This card offers 5x points for purchases made in select categories and at featured merchants that change each quarter. You can earn 5x on up to $1,500 of qualifying spending each quarter. It also offers you 3x points on dining and delivery, 3x at drugstores, and 5x on travel purchased through Chase. There's no annual fee for this card, and the only catch is that you must register online to activate the 5x promotion every quarter.

As with the Freedom Unlimited card, you can't directly transfer the points you earn from this card to travel partners, but you can combine the reward points earned from this card with points from your Chase Sapphire Preferred, Sapphire Reserve, or Ink Business Preferred. Likewise, there's no annual fee for this card.

Sapphire Preferred. This popular travel rewards card offers 3x points on dining, online grocery, and select streaming purchases.

You also receive 2x points on travel and 1 point per dollar spent elsewhere. Having this card allows you to use the points you earned with other Chase cards for transfers to airline and hotel points. This card also offers excellent shopping protection and travel insurance policies. It is well worth its $95 annual fee. This is the card that I've introduced many of my family and friends to here in Dever. Like me, they are able to transfer their rewards to the two biggest airlines in town, United and Southwest. These airlines are very complimentary, as Southwest can offer very low prices to domestic destinations, including Hawaii, and even vacation spots in Mexico and the Caribbean. United, with its worldwide network and dozens of partners, allows us to redeem our miles for flights around the world. I also recommend using this card to pay for incidental travel expenses, including rental cars and even taxes and fees on awards. When you do that, you receive perks like trip delay and trip cancellation insurance, lost and delayed baggage coverage, and primary rental car insurance.

Sapphire Reserve. This is Chase's flagship travel rewards card, and I've had it since it was first offered. It features 3x points for all travel and dining purchases. It also offers 5x points for airfare booked through Chase and 10x points for all other travel booked through Chase. It also features a Priority Pass Select membership that allows you and two guests access to the Chase airport lounge network. There's a $550 annual fee for this card but there's also a $300 annual travel credit and a $100 credit towards a Global Entry or TSA PreCheck application.

CHASE SMALL BUSINESS CARDS

Ink Business Cash. This is a no-fee card for small business owners. Although it's marketed as a cash back card, your rewards will come in the form of Chase Ultimate Rewards points. When combined with points from your Chase Sapphire Preferred, Sapphire Reserve, or Ink Business Preferred, you can transfer these points to airline and hotel travel partners.

This card earns a fantastic 5x points per dollar spent at office supply stores and on telecommunications service providers such as telephone, television, and internet providers. That means that whenever I buy something from an office supply store, such as school supplies, furniture, or gift cards, I earn five points per dollar spent. I earn 5x points for all my mobile phone and internet services. I also earn 2x points for gas purchases, which makes it the only Chase Ultimate Rewards card that offers a bonus for gas. Even when I buy a new mobile phone through my service provider, I still earn 5x. There's no annual fee for this card, which makes it an excellent choice for small business owners. It's my preferred business card and I use it for many office and business-related expenses.

Ink Business Unlimited. Like the Ink Business Cash, this card is marketed as a cash back card, however you still earn Chase Ultimate Rewards points that you can transfer to airline and hotel travel partners once you combine those points with another Chase card that features points transfers. And like the Freedom Unlimited, the Ink Unlimited offers 1.5x points per dollar spent, making it a great choice for purchases that don't earn a bonus on other cards. There's no annual fee for this card.

Ink Business Preferred. This is Chase's premium travel rewards card for small business. It offers 3x points per dollar spent on shipping purchases; advertising purchases made with social media sites and search engines; Internet, cable and phone services; and on travel. You earn 3x points on your first $150,000 spent in combined purchases in those categories each account anniversary year, and 1 point per dollar spent on all other purchases. There's a $95 annual fee for this card.

CHASE ULTIMATE REWARDS STRENGTHS

This program's strengths include its transfer partners and the numerous cards offered. The Chase transfer partners I use the most are United, Southwest, and Hyatt, which aren't available from any of the other major credit card rewards programs (with the exception of Bilt Rewards, which as I mentioned earlier in the chapter also offers United and Hyatt).

At the same time, this program makes it easy to add new credit cards to your portfolio in order to realize new account bonuses, different spending bonuses, and valuable benefits. Between my wife and I, we hold all of the cards mentioned in this section on Chase that earn Ultimate Rewards points. It took us a few years to get around to applying for all of them, but it's been worth it as we earned generous signup bonuses each time, and it's the program we rely upon the most.

I also like that you can use your Chase Ultimate Rewards points to book travel through Chase at decent rates. Sapphire Preferred and Ink Business Preferred cardholders receive a nominal 1.25 cents in value per point redeemed, while Sapphire Reserve cardholders receive a substantially better 1.5 cents in value. Neither approaches the 2 to 4 cents in value that you can sometimes get from transferring your points to travel partners and redeeming them for high-value reservations. But sometimes booking direct through Chase will make the most sense, especially for beginners who have yet to learn how to extract maximum value from their frequent flier miles or hotel points. And when you book your flights through Chase, they still earn frequent flier miles, which helps you earn or retain elite status while receiving a small rebate on your points spent.

WEAKNESSES

For all Chase's strengths, it still has a few weaknesses. For example, Chase lacks a card that offers bonus points at supermarkets, which is a glaring omission. Chase also lacks a few key transfer partners such as Avianca, which is a great Star Alliance carrier that never imposes surcharges. I also find ANA and Qantas to be great American Express Membership Rewards partners that are missing from Chase's lineup. Finally, Chase offers transfers to Marriott and IHG hotels, but only at a 1 to 1 ratio. Both Marriott and IHG points are worth far less than 1 cent each, so cardholders would be crazy to make those transfers, other than to occasionally top off their account with 1,000 or 2,000 additional points needed for an award.

WHO THE CHASE REWARDS PROGRAM IS BEST FOR

This is a great flexible travel rewards program for beginners and experienced award travel enthusiasts alike. Beginners can utilize easy programs like Southwest and Hyatt, or just redeem their points directly through Chase. More advanced award travelers can maximize partners like United, Air Canada, Virgin Atlantic, and Air France/KLM. Because its strengths apply to award travelers of all skill levels, it's rare that I meet a collector of points and miles that doesn't have a wallet full of Chase cards.

CITI THANKYOU POINTS

Citi ThankYou Points is a strong program that's been around for many years. I've taken a renewed interest in it since their credit card offerings and their list of transfer partners has grown. But you should know that most Citi Cards no longer offers any purchase protection or travel insurance benefits, although the Citi Strata Premier does. You don't even get extended warranty coverage or rental car insurance.

CITI THANKYOU POINTS PARTNERS

Airlines:

- Aeromexico Club Premier (part of the SkyTeam Alliance)
- Air France-KLM Flying Blue (part of the SkyTeam Alliance)
- Avianca LifeMiles (part of the Star Alliance)
- Cathay Pacific Asia Miles (part of the OneWorld Alliance)
- Emirates Skywards
- Etihad Guest
- Eva Air Infinity MileageLands (part of the Star Alliance)
- JetBlue TrueBlue
- Qantas Frequent Flyer (part of the OneWorld Alliance)
- Qatar Airways Privilege Club (part of the OneWorld Alliance)
- Singapore Airlines KrisFlyer(part of the Star Alliance)
- Thai Airways Royal Orchid Plus (part of the Star Alliance)
- Turkish Airlines Miles & Smiles (part of the Star Alliance)
- Virgin Atlantic Flying Club (part of the SkyTeam Alliance)

Hotels:

- Choice Privileges (transfers at a 1 to 2 ratio)

- Leaders Club (transfer at a 5 to 1 ratio)
- Wyndham Rewards

CREDIT CARDS THAT OFFER CITI THANKYOU POINTS

AT&T Points Plus℠ Card from Citi. Although co-branded with AT&T, this card offers rewards in the form of Citi ThankYou Points. You earn 3x points at gas stations, 2x at grocery stores (including delivery services) and 1point per dollar spent elsewhere. So where does AT&T come in? When you use the card to spend $1,000 during a billing cycle, you get a $20 credit towards your AT&T bill. Spend from $500 to $999.99, and you earn $10 back. So, if you are an AT&T subscriber, then you have the chance to earn something like cash back while still earning travel rewards points. Plus, there's no annual fee for this card.

Citi Custom Cash. Don't let the name fool you, this card actually offers ThankYou Points. By itself, you can't transfer these points to travel partners, but if you also have the Citi Premier, then you can. This card offers 5x points per dollar spent in your top eligible spend category, each billing cycle, for up to $500 spent. All other purchases earn one point per dollar spent, and there's no annual fee for this card.

Citi Double Cash. Like the Citi Custom Cash, this card offers its rewards in the form of ThankYou Points. And you can only transfer these points to miles if you also have the Citi Premier card. The Double Cash offers 2 points per dollar spent. Technically, you earn 1 point when you make a purchase and 1 point when you pay for a purchase. Like the Capital One Venture and Venture X cards, this is a fantastic card for non-bonus spendingwhen you can't earn 2x points with another card. There's no annual fee for this card.

Citi Rewards+. This card offers 2x points at supermarkets and gas stations on up to $6,000 in combined spending each year, and 1 point per dollar spent elsewhere. But what makes this card interesting is that Citi rounds up purchases to the nearest 10 points. So a purchase of 29 cents earns 10 points, just as a purchase of $10 would. And if you spend $10.01, you'll earn 20 points. If you make just a few large purchases, you will earn only a small benefit, but if you frequently use this card for small purchases, you could potentially earn a lot more points than you would have otherwise. There's no annual fee for this card.

Citi Strata Premier. If you're going to collect Citi ThankYou Points, then you must have this card. That's because carrying it allows you to transfer your ThankYou Points earned from other cards to airline and hotel partners. Transferring these points to airline and hotel partners and redeeming them for high-value travel reservations can offer you much more value than all of the other options, such as gift cards, cash back, and merchandise rewards that only return a maximum of 1 cent per point redeemed. I'll talk more about getting the most value for your points in Chapter 7.

Thankfully, the Citi Strata Premier is also a very competitive travel rewards card. It offers 3x points at restaurants, supermarkets, and gas stations. It also offers 3x points for air travel and hotels. There is a $95 annual fee for this card but it's worth it to allow point transfers from all of your other cards that offer Citi ThankYou Points.

CitiBusiness ThankYou® Card Rewards. This is an oddball card that few award travel enthusiasts know about. While you can find most of the cards mentioned in this book on my website, JasonSteele.com, you can only apply for this card at a Citi branch location. This card offers 3x ThankYou Points for purchases from featured merchant categories that change each quarter. These categories can include typical business purchases like office supplies, advertising, software, and dining. You earn 1 point per dollar spent elsewhere and there's no annual fee.

CITI THANKYOU STRENGTHS

As with Capital One Miles, Citi ThankYou Points has a strong list of international airline transfer partners but no domestic ones. Citi offers several compelling personal credit cards that earn ThankYou Points. Points are easy to combine and even to share or gift to others. Wyndham is a very strong hotel option that Citi ThankYou Rewards Program partners with, and Choice Hotels points transfer at a 1 to 2 ratio, which is excellent.

WEAKNESSES

- There are no transfer partners that truly stand out.
- Citi only has one small business card, and it isn't easy to use since it must be applied at a Citi branch location.
- Citi no longer offers its Prestige card to new applicants, which is a premium rewards product.

WHO CITI THANKYOU REWARDS IS BEST FOR

This is a very strong program, but it's not in the top-tier like American Express Membership Rewards or Chase Ultimate Rewards. Citi ThankYou Points compliment those programs by offering some innovative credit cards and a few transfer partners that the big ones miss, such as Turkish Airlines and Wyndham Hotels. The ability to transfer Citi ThankYou Points to Choice Hotels points at a 1 to 2 ratio also makes this program valuable.

WELLS FARGO REWARDS

Shortly before this book went to print, Wells Fargo introduced its Autograph Journey card, which offers points that can be transferred to airlines and hotels through its Rewards program.

WELLS FARGO TRANSFER PARTNERS

Airlines

- Aer Lingus AerClub (A member of OneWorld)
- Air France-KLM Flying Blue (A member of SkyTeam)
- Avianca LifeMiles (A member of the Star Alliance)
- British Airways Executive Club (A member of OneWorld)
- Iberia Plus (A member of OneWorld)

Hotel Partners

- Choice Privileges (transfers at a 1:2 ratio).

CREDIT CARDS THAT OFFER GO FAR REWARDS

For the moment, there's just the new Autograph Journey card, although there's likely to be more. And their Active Cash card offers rewards that can be combined with the Autograph Journey.

WELL FARGO STRENGTHS

- The Autograph Journey is a winner as it offers 5x points on hotels, 4x points on airlines, and 3x points on other travel and restaurants.

- Although the list of cards that offer Rewards is small, Wells Fargo offers transfer partners from each of the major alliances.
- Points transfer to Choice Hotels at a 1:2 ratio.

WEAKNESSES

- Only one card, for the moment.
- Few transfer options, but that's expected to change.

WHO WELLS FARGO GO FAR REWARDS IS BEST FOR

This new program has a lot of potential, so it's one to watch. For now it's a great way for award travel enthusiasts to diversify the types of rewards they are earning, while receiving an outstanding 5x points on hotels and 4x at restaurants.

A NOTE ABOUT MARRIOTT BONVOY

The Marriott Bonvoy program is a strange animal but one we need to look at in terms of what it can offer in the way of transferrable rewards to airlines and the Marriott hotels. Think of it as kind of like a platypus, the mammal that lays eggs. Like our furry friend from Down Under that seems to be part of two animal group, the Marriott Bonvoy rewards program is part transferrable rewards program and part hotel loyalty program.

In some ways, Marriott Bonvoy could be considered the ultimate flexible travel rewards program. It offers a whopping 39 airline transfer partners, which is several times more than any other program. And while many of them are obscure foreign carriers that provide little value, there are a few gems among them such as Alaska, American Airlines, Korean, Aegean, and Virgin Australia.

But when it comes to using it to get free hotel stays, as I mentioned in Chapter 4, Marriott isn't my favorite hotel program. That's because you can't really collect points at a competitive rate using credit cards for purchases other than Marriott hotel stays. The Marriott cards offered by both Chase and Amex offer 2 points per dollar spent. This sounds fine until you realize that points transfer to airline miles at a ratio of 3 to 1 with a bonus of 5,000 miles when you transfer 60,000 points to miles. So, for every 60,000 Marriott points you transfer, you'll receive 25,000 airline points. Do the math, and you find that for every $30,000 dollars you spend, you'll receive 25,000 airline miles, or 0.83 miles per dollar. In a world where you can effectively earn 2 miles per dollar spent from cards like the Capital One Venture, Citi Double Cash, and American Express Blue Business® Plus, earning 0.83 miles per dollar spent doesn't come close to offering competitive value.

Even though Marriott Bonvoy isn't one of my favorite hotel programs, it's still the largest and it still has millions of loyal customers. As a hotel loyalty program, Marriott Bonvoy works best for frequent Marriott guests who pay for their stays with Marriott credit cards, which have fantastic points earning power. But for people like me who just want to earn free stays by using credit cards for other purchases, the Marriott Bonvoy program just doesn't cut it.

One caveat in all this: If you already have a stash of Marriott Bonvoy points, you should be aware that they are very valuable when transferred to airline partners and redeemed for international business class reservations at the lowest mileage rates available.

CHAPTER 5 CASE STUDY: CONSIDER THE VARIABLES

One of my clients, Ajeet, lives in the northeast corner of Washington State and travels for work and pleasure throughout the West Coast, and a little bit internationally. But his trips are mostly in support of his company that produces jewelry he sells online.

Ajeethad been using a United Airlines credit card and had earned 310,000 miles from using that card but was only earning one mile per dollar spent on most purchases. He also carried a Delta SkyMiles Platinum card and earned 210,000 miles from it. Finally, he had an Alaska Airlines credit card, from which he earned 100,000 miles.

Altogether, this was a mishmash of different credit card strategies, and my goal was to find one or two that would work the best for him. His closest airport is in Bellingham, Washington near the Canadian border. Bellingham Airport, while being convenient it's very small, with service on Alaska Airlines to Seattle, and Southwest Airlines to Denver, Las Vegas and Oakland. When I found that many of his business and personal trips were to Las Vegas, I recommended that he get both a business and personal credit card from Southwest in order to earn their Companion Pass. These two cards would offer him nearly $2,000 of points, which would be worth double that when he adds a companion, for a mere $5.60 in taxes per flight. And by flying out of Bellingham to Las Vegas instead of spending several hours driving down to Seattle to fly from there, he was able to conveniently and easily hop on a plane closest to his home, saving drive time and expensive long-term airport parking fees.(Sadly, Southwest has since ceased flying to Bellinghan, but Ajeet can still use his points to fly on Southwest from Seattle.)

I also recommended that he get the Chase Ink Business Preferred card, as it was offering a sign-up bonus of 100,000 points at the time, and those points could be transferred to numerous partners including Southwest, United, and Hyatt. Another suggestion was that he compliment the Chase Ink Business Preferred with the Ink Business Unlimited, which offers 1.5 points per dollar spent on everything, and those points could be combined with the Chase Ink Business Preferred and transferred to airlines and hotels.

Ajeet had been using AirBnB instead of staying in hotels, but I explained how he could transfer his Chase points to Hyatt and stay there for free. When I showed him all of the Hyatt hotels that he could stay in for a reasonable number of points, he loved this idea. Finally, I suggested he and his wife consider eventually adding a business or personal Alaska card to their wallets, if only to get the sign-up bonus. As Alaska is the dominant carrier in his home airport of Bellingham, and the next closest airports are in Everett and Seattle, he couldn't go wrong with this, especially as I showed him Alaska's numerous airline partners that he could redeem his miles with.

I also recommended that he close his Delta SkyMiles Platinum card when the annual fee came due. Not only are Delta SkyMiles worth less than most airline miles, this card has a very high annual fee. I also urged him to downgrade his United card to a no-fee version. This will allow him to continue to be a United cardholder and enjoy the ability to book award seats for fewer miles than non-cardholders can.

The lessons here are that your choice of a credit card strategy will often depend on where you live, what your closest airport is, *and what destinations you frequent. Since Ajeet's local airport had better service on Southwest than other airlines, and his frequent destinations had affordable Hyatt hotels, it made sense to choose a credit card strategy that focused on earning Chase Ultimate Rewards points. Unlike other credit cards, these points can be transferred to both Southwest and Hyatt. And if he earned some Alaska miles from other credit cards, that could meet his international travel needs.*

I ended the consultation, as I always like to do with all my clients, by helping Ajeet realize that he should be able to earn enough points for all of his airfare and hotel needs going forward, and that he will rarely, if ever, have to pay for travel again.

IN CONCLUSION...

In the first part of the book, I introduced the basic concepts of award travel. And in this second part, I gave you a tour of all the major airline, hotel, and credit card rewards programs. Now comes the fun part, as we put it all together in Part 3 to show you how you can use this information to start traveling for free! But before going on, please be sure to complete the challenge that follows for Chapter 5.

CHAPTER 5 CHALLENGE:

1. Which credit card rewards programs do you currently participate in?

2. Do you carry all of the best cards currently offered to earn rewards in those programs?

3. Are there other programs that might better meet your needs, or complement the programs that you already use?

PART 3:

Earning and Redeeming the Most Rewards –
Plus, Recipes for Creating Exciting Award Travel Adventures

In Part 1 I introduced you to the world of award travel and all its exciting possibilities. In Part 2 I showed you all of the best ways to earn the points and miles that you can use to take advantage of award travel. In fact, you can think of these rewards as the ingredients that you'll need to travel for free. In Part 3 I'm going to explain how to earn and redeem the most amount of rewards possible, plus, I will share specific instructions — "recipes" so to speak — that will show you simple and easy ways to put all the information from earlier chapters together to plan and experience exciting award travel adventures.

CHAPTER 6:

Earning as Many Points and Miles as Possible

✈────────────────

If you're a dentist, you probably notice everyone's smile. If you work in the automotive industry, I'm sure you pay attention to the cars your friends drive. As I became more and more of a travel and credit card expert, I realized that I was noticing the cards my friends and family members were using to pay their dinner bill and judging them whenever it came time to split the check when we went out to eat.

Maybe it shouldn't have surprised me, but I found that most of my friends and family members weren't choosing their method of payment based on the value of the points and miles they could earn. Instead, most would pay with the same credit card they had been using for years. And to my shock and horror, some even used debit cards, which offer no rewards at all! From my perspective they might as well have been using $10 bills as tissues with which to blow their nose, and then throwing them away!

Paying for a dinner bill is just one small way to earn points and miles. But in order to earn the most travel rewards, you must focus on several different methods for earning points and miles, including signing up for new credit cards, using the right cards for each purchase, and taking advantage of the numerous additional opportunities available. I like to think of this as gathering all the right "ingredients" needed to create the best award travel trips possible. Just as you need to shop for ingredients before you can start cooking, you'll need to "gather" your points and miles before you can start booking reward travel. In this chapter, I'll show you how to earn the most points and miles and in Chapter 7, I'll share the most efficient way to redeem all those points you've worked so hard to earn, plus some of my favorite "recipes" that I use to turn those rewards into free travel.

GATHERING THE RIGHT INGREDIENTS

Imagine you are visiting a friend's house and are asked to prepare a meal. The first thing you'd probably do is go to the kitchen and inventory what's there, and what you can use. You'd also want to make a shopping list of what you are missing so you could make a trip to the grocery store. This chapter is about getting very familiar with knowing how to gather the ingredients you need and in the right amounts in preparation for pulling together exciting award travel "dishes."

I've broken down the easiest and most efficient ways to earn the most "ingredients" (points and miles) into three primary methods:

1. Earning credit card new account bonuses;
2. Optimizing credit card spending; and
3. Taking advantage of promotions.

EARN LOTS OF POINTS WITH CREDIT CARD SIGNUP BONUSES

The credit card industry is both extremely competitive and highly profitable, at the same time. This rare combination creates the perfect conditions for credit card issuers to offer very generous bonuses to new account holders. For that reason, opening a new credit card account is one of the easiest ways to gather the ingredients necessary for creating the best free travel adventures and why I advise my clients to focus on this first.

In the past, earning credit card sign up bonuses wasn't necessarily the best way to accrue miles quickly since it was common to receive just 25,000 airline miles when you opened a new credit card account. Back then, you could only redeem those miles for a domestic, round-trip ticket in economy class. But today, it's rare to see an airline credit card offering less than 50,000 miles, and offers of 75,000, 100,000 miles, or more are common. With generic travel rewards credit cards, such as the Chase Sapphire Preferred or Capital One Venture Rewards cards, you typically see offers of 75,000 points or miles or more. I've even found some of the most generous offers for American Express Platinum cards at 100,000 to as much as 150,000 points.

The beauty of earning travel rewards this way is how quick it is. It takes just seconds to apply for a card, and you can earn these bonuses just by purchasing things you would have bought anyway. In the past, when airlines offered one frequent flyer mile per mile traveled, it would take about an hour in the air to earn just 500 miles, or two days straight of flying around the world to earn 25,000 miles Yet I can earn over 100,000 miles in a matter of seconds just by opening a new credit card account. In fact, I wouldn't take a free ticket if it were offered to me as it wouldn't be worth my time to fly around the world just to earn a mere 25,000 miles.

When people learn that credit card issuers are handing out massive amounts of travel rewards just for signing up for a credit card, they may wonder why everyone doesn't just run out and open dozens of new accounts every year. There are a few reasons why it's best to moderate the volume of your credit card applications.

First, all of these offers will have minimum spending requirements. For example, a credit card might offer new applicants 75,000 miles but only after they use their card to spend $4,000 within three months of opening the account. Those six-figure sign-up bonuses on American Express Platinum cards, for instance, can require you to spend as much as $15,000 on the card within three months of account opening. Needless to say, this can be beyond the means of many credit card users.

The second reason why you shouldn't open a ton of new accounts, as I have tried to stress throughout this book, is because you *must* be able to responsibly manage all of your credit cards in order to play the travel-for-free game, which can be a challenge for some people. You need to know yourself and your spending habits. As an expert in credit cards and consumer credit, I'm frequently asked how many cards a person should have. As I noted in the Introduction, my answer is always, "No more than you can manage responsibly." But if you avoid overspending and debt and pay your bills on time, then there's no reason that you can't have numerous cards. Janna and I each currently have over 20 open accounts each. We spend money on these cards in the same way we would use cash, and we avoid interest by always paying our

balances in full and on time. In fact, we use the card's autopay feature to ensure that we are never making a late payment, even when we're traveling or occupied with other parts of life.

WAIT FOR THE BEST OFFERS, THEN POUNCE!

When you take a safari in Africa, you'll notice most of the animals stand around grazing on the grass. Then there are others that lurk in the bush, waiting for the right prey to walk by. When it comes to applying for new credit cards, let's just say that I prefer the latter approach. Instead of applying for every card we see, my wife and I prefer to wait for the best offers and then pounce on them. This is always the best way to find the most valuable offers, especially when you consider that many credit card issuers now have limits to the number of new account bonuses that you can earn. For example, Chase has an unpublished rule, known informally as 5-24, that will deny new accounts to anyone who has opened five or more personal credit cards in the previous 24 months. New small business cards don't count towards 5-24, but you can't be approved for a business card if you are over 5-24. American Express has a once-per-lifetime rule on most of its cards. This means that you won't qualify for a new account bonus if you've had that same card at some point in the past. Thankfully, American Express now lets you know if you'll qualify for the signup bonus, before you submit your application.

DON'T CLOSE NEW ACCOUNTS SHORTLY AFTER OPENING THEM

Even though I open up a few new card accounts each year, the last thing I would ever do is close the account shortly after receiving the signup bonus. To me, applying for a new card and ac-cepting the new account bonus creates an informal agreement between me and the issuer to give the new card a try. That's why I'll always keep the card for a year before deciding whether or not it meets my needs going forward. In fact, when I first applied for the premium Chase Sapphire Reserve card, I did so primarily to earn the new account bonus. However, I later found tremendous value in the card, decided to keep it, and have been using it for many years. It's one of my favorites. But if this reasoning doesn't sway your opinion, you should also know that card issuers frown on customers who receive generous sign-up bonuses just before canceling their cards. American Express, in particular, includes language in their cardholder agreement giving them the right to revoke bonus points from those who cancel their cards within the first year. And since you can always cancel your card after one year, before paying your account's annual fee again, there's sim-ply no reason to cancel it earlier and risk damaging your relation-ship with a major credit card issuer.

So back to the question about how many new cards to sign up for. As I said, this is totally dependent on how well you can manage them, if you can control your spending and debt, pay your balance on time every month, and whether you can commit to giving the card a good try by keeping it for at least a year. So, the short answer is, it depends — each household is different. In my case, I usually sign up for three or four new credit cards a year. That way I can easily earn 400,000 to 500,000 points or miles. And in our family, my wife and I work in what some call "two-player mode." So, when Janna signs up for a similar number of cards, we

can earn nearly a million points every year, just from these new account bonuses.

When I speak to award travel consulting clients who are new to earning points and miles, I often have to get them started earning rewards from credit cards. The goal is to get them started with large signup bonuses, as well as to build the portfolio of plastic that they'll be able to use in the long-term. When working with a couple, I'll usually have them both apply for one or two cards each, depending on how easily they can meet each card's minimum spending requirement.

While earning credit card signup bonuses is a major part of the strategy I use in coaching my clients, I don't encourage this nearly as aggressively as some other award travel experts do. I have never signed up for dozens of credit cards in a year, so I certainly don't recommend that others do, as you should never have more cards than you can manage responsibly. And as my portfolio of plastic increases beyond manageable levels, I will regularly re-evaluate which ones continue to offer me value going forward. If the cost of the annual fee doesn't justify the benefits received, then I will cancel the card. These regular purges allow me to hold just the cards I need, which is usually around 20.

By applying for new cards in moderation, most of my clients can still earn several hundred thousand miles each year in signup bonuses alone. I'm always happy to conclude my consultations by showing my clients how they'll never have to pay for travel again if they use the methods I teach about how to earn and redeem the most points and miles possible.

EARN MORE POINTS BY OPTIMIZING YOUR SPENDING

As I mentioned at the beginning of this chapter, it is always baffling to me to see the way some people use their cards that does nothing for optimizing the amount of reward points and miles that can be earned. If you want to gather as many rewards as possible in preparation for cooking up some amazing award travel you must take a good look at the way you spend using those credit cards you have signed up for. In the 2009 classic movie *Up in the Air,* George Clooney portrays a business traveler who proclaims: "I don't spend a nickel, if I can help it, unless it somehow profits my mileage account." While I wouldn't take it that far, I would rephrase Clooney's comment this way: "I don't spend a dollar without using a credit card that will offer me the most valuable points or miles for the purchase."

So how does this work?

My wife and I make it easy on ourselves by breaking that spending down into three categories and carrying only the cards needed for that spending in our purse or wallet:

1. One card is used for groceries and dining;
2. Another card is used for gas; and
3. A third card for travel purchases.

I also have a card that I use for office supplies and telecommunications spending and another for all the purchases that don't earn any bonus on any card that I have. The rest of my cards that are used for needs other than food, gas, and travel I keep at home so I'm not carrying around a stack of cards in my wallet.

Here's how it breaks down for us currently:

Dining. I'll use either my American Express Gold card, which offers 4x Membership Rewards points per dollar at restaurants or my Chase Sapphire Reserve or Freedom Unlimited, both of which offer me 3x Ultimate Rewards points per dollar spent. I find three Chase Ultimate Rewards points to be worth approximately the same as four American Express Membership Rewards points.

Groceries. I most frequently use my American Express Gold card, which offers 4x Membership Rewards points at U.S. supermarkets, on up to $25,000 spent each year. I might also use my Citi Strata Premier card, which earns 3x ThankYou Points at grocery stores.

Gas. I really like my Wyndham Rewards Business Earner card, which offers an outstanding 8x points at gas stations. I might also consider my Citi Premier card, which earns 3x ThankYou Points.

Office supplies. The Chase Ink Business Cash card offers 5x points per dollar spent at office supply stores such as Office Depot and Staples. This is where I buy gift cards from Amazon and others in order to earn 5x points for a variety of purchases. Need a new fridge? Then just buy $1,000 worth of gift cards for Lowes or The Home Depot. Just note that this card is marketed as a cash back card, but you earn points that can be transferred to your Chase Sapphire Preferred or Sapphire Reserve card, and then transferred to airline and hotel partners.

Telecommunications. The Chase Ink Business Cash card also offers 5x points per dollar spent on internet, cable, and phone services each account anniversary year.

For what I would call non-bonus spending, which are any purchases outside of these categories, I'll use my Chase Freedom

Unlimited to earn 1.5x points per dollar spent. Like the Chase Ink Business Cash card, the Freedom Unlimited is marketed as a cash back card, but you earn points that can be transferred to your Chase Sapphire Preferred or Sapphire Reserve card, and then transferred to airline and hotel partners. The Chase Ink Business Unlimited is nearly identical to the card offered to small business owners. Non-bonus spending can include purchases from home improvement stores, department stores, automotive repair places, and the like.

Another great alternative for non-bonus spending is the Capital One Venture and Venture X. Both of these cards offer double miles on all purchases. Finally, the Citi Double Cash offers 2x ThankYou Points per dollar spent, and those who also have a Citi Strata Premier card can transfer those points to travel partners.

But optimizing my credit card spending goes beyond just choosing the best credit card for each purchase. It also means simply using cards whenever possible, instead of other methods of payment. So, before I write a check or send money electronically, I always find out if I can use my credit card. For instance, you might find that you can use your credit card for utilities, insurance, health care, home improvement, and even school tuition. I love the fact that I can use a credit card to pay both my home insurance and car insurance, without incurring any additional fees. My property tax bill can be paid with a credit card, and I'll often pay my IRS tax bill with a card, even though I'll incur a "convenience fee" of about 1.8 percent. I don't enjoy paying that fee, but it's worth it when I need to reach a minimum spending requirement to earn a signup bonus. And when it came time to pay for my daughter's summer

camp, I was able to have the credit card fee waived if I paid the entire amount up-front

I'll admit that all of this spending optimization may seem like a lot to keep track of, and initially it may feel like that since you will need to become very aware of how each card that you hold works and what value it can add to your spending. This is when many people stop me and say, "Hold on, how am I supposed to keep track of all these accounts and carry all these cards around with me?" — all they can envision is the bulging "George Costanza wallet" from *Seinfeld* that seemed to hold all of George's life's possessions!

While these are legitimate concerns, I help my clients see that having these credit cards need not be a big burden. Keep in mind that in practice, I simply carry around no more than the three or four credit cards that I use for 99 percent of my most common purchases, which, as I explained earlier are for dining, groceries, and gas. I think of my wallet as a tool belt that I carry with me to get the immediate "purchasing" job done. And like any handyman, I have plenty of other tools (the other cards I need for the not-so-frequent transactions) that I keep in my tool chest back home and which I don't take with me to every job.

As I write this, in my wallet I have my American Express Gold card that I use to earn 4x points at restaurants and at grocery stores, my Chase Sapphire Reserve that I use to earn 3x for all travel purchases (and enjoy robust travel insurance protection), and I have my Chase Freedom Unlimited to earn 1.5x points on all purchases that don't qualify for the dining, grocery, or travel bonuses. With just those three cards, along with my driver's license, I don't even need to carry a wallet at all, I just use a mobile phone case that holds those four cards.

And what about all of my other cards? I have a travel wallet that's just for the cards which I use to get into airport lounges, or when I'm staying at a specific hotel. This travel wallet contains cards like my Hyatt card, my American Express Platinum, the Capital One Venture X, and the Priority Pass benefit card. And in my office, I keep a folder (which I purchased for just a few dollars at an office supply store that's specifically designed to hold credit cards) to organize my business cards that I primarily use to pay for small business purchases, taxes, utilities, and other such purposes.

Another question I hear frequently is, "How do you keep straight which of the cards in your wallet you should use for what?" As I noted in Chapter 2, an easy way to do this is to simply put a piece of masking tape on the part of the card that sticks out of your wallet and label it with its purpose, such as "Groceries," "Gas," or "Dining." If you want to get more sophisticated, there are apps such as Travel Freely or the TPG app from The Points Guy that can help you keep track of your cards, when you use them, and the amounts you spend.

BE AWARE OF THE CREDIT CARD FEES

While organizing your credit card accounts so that you are using your cards in the best way possible to earn the most amount of points, there is a downside to paying for everything with a credit card that you need to be aware of. Many merchants now days insist on adding a "credit card surcharge" of up to 5 percent onto your purchase. While it might be worth it to pay a nominal fee of

1 or 2 percent, nothing more than that makes sense. Many merchant fees for accepting credit cards are usually between 2 and 3 percent. I think up to 2 is fine but 3 percent is pushing it for me and I prefer not to do business with a company that attempts to gain a profit off their credit card surcharge.

On the other hand, you'd be surprised how often you can negotiate the use of a credit card with no surcharge. For example, whenever I purchase a car from a dealer, I first negotiate the best price I can. When I feel like the dealer won't go any lower, I then agree to the purchase on the condition that I'm able to use my credit card. I'm always told no, and my reply is always the same, "I understand, I'll just buy the car from someone else." Predictably, the salesperson doesn't like that idea, talks to his or her manager, and then agrees to make a "one time exception." I've done this multiple times, and it always works.

The goal is to get in the mindset that every time you use your travel rewards credit card, you're getting a significant discount on your purchase in the form of beneficial points and miles. And by using the right credit card, you can earn the most valuable rewards possible. Eventually, your vigilance becomes habit, and the payoff comes when you have enough of the right "ingredients" (points and miles) needed to cook up your next big trip.

TAKE ADVANTAGE OF PROMOTIONS TO INCREASE YOUR AWARD BALANCES

While the first of my two primary methods for earning the most credit card rewards, sign-up bonuses and optimized spending, are pretty straightforward, this third one is kind of a grab bag of random offers. For example, American Express frequently offers their cardholders 5,000, 10,000, or even 20,000 Membership Rewards points for adding an authorized user who will spend at $2,000 within three months. American Express can also offer its cardholders 20,000 points for enabling "Pay Over Time," which is a program that allows their charge card holders to carry a balance. You don't actually have to extend your payments out (and incur interest charges) to get this bonus, you just have to opt in to the program. In fact, you can later opt out and get the same offer over and over again.

Other credit card issuers will occasionally offer targeted spending bonuses. For example, you may get an offer that gives you 5x points per dollar spent on travel or grocery purchases for the next three months. I frequently see these offers for Chase like the ones co-branded with Southwest, Hyatt, and United. These offers are intended to entice you to start regularly using a card that you haven't spent much on lately.

Then there are merchant- specific offers. Many credit cards offer an online shopping portal that gives you bonus points. For instance, you may receive 5x points per dollar spent when you go to a particular merchant's website before making a purchase. American Express offers work like this. While you don't need to go through their shopping portal, you will need to opt in to specific offers for your account.

If you're wondering how to get the most possible points or miles from a promotion, then you can use sites like EVreward. com, which lists all of the different offers available from various airline and hotel sites, depending on the merchant. For example, a purchase from popular retailers like Petco or The Home Depot might earn 2x American Airlines miles, 5x United Miles or 3

percent cash back, depending on which portal you used. You simply choose the one that's most valuable to you.

There's also dining rewards programs that give you additional bonus points for making purchases from specific restaurants. To receive this, you simply enroll your card into the program and you'll automatically earn points or miles. These dining rewards programs are available from numerous airline and hotel programs. Since there's no cost to add your credit cards to these dining portals, and there's nothing additional that you need to do to earn points when you dine, this is an easy way to earn points without thinking about it.

I could probably include several chapters on these kinds of promotions, but many would be out of date by the time of publishing. However, you should make it a point to go to the websites of your favorite airline, hotel, and credit card rewards programs and familiarize yourself with all of the offers available. Each one by itself might not make a huge difference in the number of points or miles you earn, but the overall effect can be very significant.

WRAPPING UP YOUR SHOPPING TRIP

So, now you're just about ready to exit the grocery store and get ready to cook up some amazing vacations. But before we start, let's get an idea of how this "grocery shopping" for enough of the right "ingredients" works in practice.

Let's say that a couple starts earning miles by signing up for credit cards (nothing too radical, like signing up for a dozen cards at once or anything, but just one per quarter). If you're both acting like the predators lurking in the bush, and your average signup bonus is 75,000 points or miles, you'll both earn 600,000 miles a year, which is pretty good by itself.

Then, let's say that you two spend $60,000 on your credit cards, but you optimize your spending so that you earn an average of two points or miles per dollar spent. This should be pretty easy to achieve as there are plenty of cards that offer as much as 2x on all purchases and up to a 5x bonus for purchases from specific categories of merchants. Now you've earned another 120,000 points or miles. Stay vigilant looking for promotions for bonus miles, adding additional authorized users to your accounts, or making purchases from specific merchants, and you should be able to earn another 80,000 points or miles. Now you're earning 800,000 points or miles a year!

As I have noted previously, when I show my clients how this is possible, we usually end the meeting by concluding that they will never have to pay for travel again. Earning 800,000 points or miles annually is enough for them to take a range of trips each year. In my case, these many points and miles allow me to travel for all the business I need each year, to take two or three domestic family vacations, and to go ona big international trip with my family — in business class mind you. These rewards cover the cost of airfare and hotel reservations, and I only pay a small amount in taxes and fees. The extra taxes and fees are typically $5.60 per flight domestically, and an average of about $100 per flight internationally.

CHAPTER 6 CASE STUDY: STARTING FROM SCRATCH AND ENDING UP IN BUSINESS CLASS

When I first started writing full-time in 2011, the first thing I did was to rent office space nearby so I could be away from the dis-

tractions at home. That's when I met Lee and Mary Williams, and I've been sharing office space with them and their adult children ever since. Lee and Mary are very successful small business owners, in the real estate and insurance businesses respectively, but they hadn't thought much about traveling overseas or using credit card rewards, until they heard about my travels and my work.

Eventually, they wanted to try out my techniques for earning and spending points and miles, and I was happy to offer my advice. Soon Mary had applied for both the Chase Sapphire Preferred, with an 80,000-point bonus, and the Chase Ink Business Unlimited, with a 100,000-point bonus. Lee also applied for the Chase Ink Business Unlimited as well an American Express Business Platinum card.

Once they met the minimum spending requirements for their cards, they had several hundred thousand points to spend. Lee and Mary decided that they wanted to travel to Spain, where Mary had been born when her father was serving in the military. I showed them how they could transfer Mary's and Lee's points from their Ink Business Preferred cards to Mary's Sapphire Preferred. I then found them two, round-trip business-class tickets from Denver to Spain.

They transferred their points to United to book their trip on a combination of flights from United and their partners. Their itinerary took them from Denver to Chicago on United, then on to Zurich in the opulent Swiss business class before the short flight to Barcelona. After touring Spain for two weeks, with their hotels largely paid for with points, they returned from Madrid, via Brussels Belgium and Chicago in Brussels Airline business class, and back to Denver on United. They returned to tell me they had *the time of their lives, and they are now looking forward to their next trip to Africa, paying for it once again with their credit card rewards.*

BOTTOM LINE...

When people first hear about trips like the Williams are now taking and of all my travels, including business-class travel overseas and luxury hotel stays, most people imagine that we are either fantastically wealthy, incredibly wasteful, or both. Having maintained this lifestyle sustainably, for over 15 years, and paying just a small amount on travel taxes and fees and credit card annual fees, I can tell you that I'm neither wealthy nor wasteful. In fact, I'm still the extremely frugal guy who will often take public transportation to the airport before boarding my business-class flights overseas.

In the next chapter, I'll show you how to take the points and miles you're earning — the recipe ingredients we've been shopping for in this chapter — to cook up some free and easy travel opportunities like those I take with my family and those the Williams are enjoying all over the world. Before going on, be sure to complete the challenge for this chapter.

CHAPTER 6 CHALLENGE:

1. What are the best credit card offers available now? (Hint: I keep a list at JasonSteele.com/cards).
2. Can you easily meet the minimum spending requirements of these offers?
3. Which ones have the best combination of rewards and benefits, and could be useful long-term additions to your wallet?

CHAPTER 7:

Recipes for Creating Exciting Award Travel

In Chapter 6 we covered the three ways to quickly and efficiently earn the most points and miles needed to be sure you have enough to book award travel: 1) earning large credit card sign-up bonuses; 2) optimizing your credit card spending; and 3) taking advantage of promotions. In this chapter, I will use these three methods to show you how to follow sample travel "recipes" we will cover. To take the cooking analogy a bit further and before we can get into creating our free travel "dishes," we also need to discuss how to best redeem all the travel reward ingredients you have gathered.

TRANSFERRING: THE BEST WAY TO REDEEM POINTS AND MILES

I always tell people that how you redeem your points and miles is at least as important as how you earn them. That's because I see so many people efficiently earning plenty of points using the methods we discussed in the last chapter but redeeming those points very inefficiently. Here are some examples of what I mean by this: Most credit card reward programs will offer you a mere one cent per point or mile towards travel reservations booked through its travel agency, which is not a great value. Programs like this include American Express Membership Rewards, Capital One Miles, and Citi ThankYou Points. While Chase will give Sapphire Preferred cardholders a marginally better 1.25 cents per point and Sapphire Reserve cardholders can redeem their points for travel reservations at a more reasonable rate of 1.5 cents per point, but you are still not realizing as much travel value as you could. And when you simply redeem your points for merchandise, such as gift cards or cash back instead of travel rewards, you will typically receive one cent in value per point redeemed, at most.

But when you *transfer* your flexible rewards to travel providers and redeem those points or miles for high-value options for business-class international flights and free hotel awards during peak season, it's often possible to receive two or more cents in value per point redeemed. For instance, Chase Ultimate Rewards points transfer to Southwest Rapid Rewards at a 1 to 1 ratio, and Southwest points are worth about 1.4 cents each, which is a decent value. But I can do even better when I transfer those points to the World of Hyatt program, where I frequently receive 2 or 3 cents in value per point, which is much better. Additionally, when I'm able to transfer my points to airline miles and redeem those miles for business-class flights overseas at the lowest mileage levels offered, it's not uncommon for me to receive 3 to 5 cents in value. So, let's say that I transfer 120,000 Chase Ultimate Rewards points to the United MileagePlus program — I would then redeem

those points for a round-trip, business-class ticket to Europe that sells for $5,000. If you do the math, you can see that I am realizing over four cents in value per point redeemed. When I transfer and redeem my points in this way, it's easy for me to choose a business-class ticket to Europe, for instance, over $1,200 in gift cards, cash back, or merchandise. Having redeemed millions of points and miles for business-class international awards in the past, my choice is clear... I will always transfer points and miles so I can earn free travel. Sure, some will argue that you aren't actually saving $5,000, since few frugal travel rewards enthusiasts would ever consider paying that much money for a few hours in the premium cabin of an airplane, no matter how luxurious. I get that. However, those business class flights have changed my entire travel experience, and earning those coveted seats is for me and my family has become the primary goal of my award travel activities. Even redeeming points for economy class international tickets can still provide strong value, especially when traveling during peak seasons.

A FEW SAMPLE RECIPES FOR CREATING FREE TRAVEL

Now that you understand the importance of earning plenty of points and miles (shopping for and gathering enough ingredients, see Chapter 6) and redeeming your travel rewards efficiently (having the right high-value items to "cook" with, which we just covered) let me offer you some examples of how to cook with these ingredients, using what I'll call "travel recipes."

Before you can start cooking, however, you need to take stock of the ingredients you put in your pantry after your grocery shopping trip... make a list of your household credit cards and their rewards balances. With the information you learned in Chapter 5 on flexible travel rewards programs like American Express Membership Rewards, Chase Ultimate Rewards, Capital One Miles, Bilt Rewards, Citi ThankYou points, and Wells Fargo Go Far points, be sure to pay special attention to these balances. Next, list the rewards that you have with airline and hotel programs. It can be helpful to use a free tool called Award Wallet to keep track of your balances of points and miles, as well as your login; other apps that you can use to track balances include Travel Freely and the TPG app.

With those balances in hand you're ready to begin cooking by deciding where you want to go and by following a good recipe for booking that travel. Thankfully I have a few easy ones to get you started.

RECIPE 1: DOMESTIC TRIP (WORKS FOR MEXICO AND THE CARIBBEAN AS WELL!)

This is how I create my most common award trip. It's a really easy travel "recipe" as it uses two of the simplest travel rewards programs.

Ingredients:

1. Chase Ultimate Rewards points
2. Substitutions: Southwest Rapid Rewards and World of Hyatt points

How to prepare:

If you have Chase Ultimate Rewards points, you can easily transfer them to Southwest Rapid Rewards points and World of Hyatt

points. But you can use up any pre-existing balances of airline miles or hotel points, if you have them.

Step 1: Find your flights.

Decide where you are going and begin pricing the award flights on Southwest's website. Make sure to consider alternate airports, as Southwest can fly to numerous airports in the same metro area, such as Los Angeles International, Burbank, and Long Beach. Thankfully, Southwest now allows you to include nearby airports in your searches.

If you have a Southwest Companion Pass, then you can save even more points on your reservation. Another strategy is to choose their "Wanna Get Away Plus" fares, which cost about 10 percent more than their standard "Wanna Get Away" fares. The advantage is that you can make same-day confirmed changes with "Wanna Get Away Plus" fares. This can allow you to save points by booking a cheaper flight as a "Wanna Get Away Plus" ticket, but potentially change it to a more expensive and desirable flight on the day of departure. Southwest allows same-day confirmed changes on Wanna Get Away Plus fares, starting at midnight.

Step 2: Find a Hyatt hotel.

It's easy to find a Hyatt hotel in most large and medium-sized cities in the U.S., but you might come up empty in smaller markets. As I have noted in previous chapters, I'm a huge fan of Hyatt Place hotels, as they offer free breakfast and tend to cost just 5,000 to 15,000 points per night. These properties typically offer rooms with two beds and a fold-out sofa, perfect for my family of five. The Hyatt House brand is similar and includes a small kitchen.

But the Hyatt brand you choose will depend on its location, its price in points, and the number of travelers in your group.

No matter what brand of Hyatt hotel that you stay in, you'll always receive waived resort fees on award stays. Additionally, if you have Globalist status with Hyatt, then you'll always receive free breakfast and free parking on award stays as well as a 4 p.m. late checkout. Earning Globalist status requires 60-night-stay credits in a calendar year, which you can get through any combination of paid stays, award stays, and night-stay credits received from their credit cards.

Step 3: Transfer the points.

Once you've confirmed award pricing and availability with both Hyatt and Southwest, transfer your Chase points to get you just the needed number of points with both programs. So, if you need 20,000 Southwest points and you already have 2,000 in your account, just transfer the 18,000 needed to book your award. This way, you keep the maximum number of points with Chase Ultimate Rewards, where you can transfer them to any of their travel partners the next time you are planning award travel.

Step 4: Book your awards.

Transfers of points from Chase Ultimate Rewards to Southwest and Hyatt occur within seconds, but you'll usually need to log out and log back in before you can see them. As soon as the points are in your account, book your awards. Don't wait! Award availability can change any second. Too often I've heard of travelers putting off their award bookings until the next day, only to find out

that the price had changed, or their room or flight was no longer available at all!

Step 5: Finish the trip.

Once you have your flights and hotels booked, then it becomes easy to figure out your remaining travel details, like ground transportation, meals, and activities. For a business trip, I might plan most details in advance, but I'll let a lot of it be spontaneous if I'm going on a vacation.

RECIPE 2: TRIP TO EUROPE

This is a more challenging recipe, as award seats to Europe can be very hard to come by during peak times. *When booking an overseas award trip, having flexible travel rewards points becomes essential to finding the best deals.* This is especially true when you are flying in international business class.

Ingredients;

1. Flexible rewards points such as Chase Ultimate Rewards, Amex Membership Rewards, Citi ThankYou Points, Wells Fargo Go Far points and Capital One Miles.
2. Award search tools such as Point.me or Seats.aero. (Alternatively, you can do this on your own so long as you have plenty of patience for searching individual airline websites.)
3. Hotel points that work well in Europe. (I'll review a few of these further into this recipe.)

HOW TO PREPARE:

Step 1: Book intercontinental airline awards.

Booking an award flight to Europe can range from easy to extremely challenging. It can be helpful to think of your trip to Europe as a Thanksgiving dinner, where the international flights are Turkey, the main dish around which everything else is built.

The challenging part about booking international award flights comes into play if you are making reservations for a large group, you don't have very flexible travel dates, and if you can't book as far as possible in advance. Thus, if you can, try to plan a European trip well in advance and try to be flexible. Think of it this way: If you are working on preparing Thanksgiving dinner, for instance, you don't wait until the last minute to start thinking about cooking the turkey. Cooking up this European free travel recipe for a single person or two passengers can be fairly easy, but for larger groups, you will need more preparation time.

What's great about international travel for larger groups is that there will often be plenty of awards available, especially if the group is traveling in economy class and during the off-season. Booking intercontinental awards to places like Europe is also easier when you book as far in advance as possible. Nearly all airlines allow you to book awards 11 months out, so that can be the ideal time to do it. That said, it will be very difficult, if not impossible to book two award tickets to Europe in business class during the summer peak season if you do it less than a few months in advance. And even when you are booking your tickets 11 months out, it can be very hard to find more than four or more business-class seats available at the lowest mileage levels. That's why it makes more

sense when following this recipe to not try to double or triple it, so to speak, just "cook" in smaller batches and serve less people if possible.

Even though free trips to Europe are harder to put together than domestic travel, you can't learn to get really good at booking them unless you practice, so begin with your favorite award program, i.e. the one where you have the most points or miles. If you have lots of miles with a specific airline, start by searching their website for awards. Always begin with the award you want on the day you want but be skeptical that you'll actually find it. Instead, try to be flexible and consider a range of dates. Also, when traveling on an international award, in order to take advantage of rewards, consider accepting the slight inconvenience of having to change planes. Using Janna and me as an example, if a non-stop flight is offered but isn't available for a reasonable number of miles, then we'll gladly take one with a change of planes. If it's always necessary to change planes to get to a particular destination, then she and I are willing to consider an itinerary with two stops so that we can travel for free. And if we're fortunate enough to be traveling in business class for free, then we won't think twice about it.

I will caution here that if you're booking your trip with points from a flexible credit card rewards program like Chase Ultimate Rewards or American Express Membership Rewards, then the recipe can become even more complicated. You essentially have to consider transferring your points to miles with each of the program's airline partners and look up potential awards with each of them. While Chase Ultimate Rewards has numerous airline partners, for example, that will get you to Europe — such as AerLingus, AerClub, Air Canada Aeroplan, Air France-KLM Flying

Blue, British Airways Executive Club, Emirates Skywards, Iberia Plus, Singapore Airlines KrisFlyer, United MileagePlus and Virgin Atlantic Flying Club — searching for awards on all of these airlines can take a lot of time. There are, however, a few tricks you can use to make this whole process easier:

Search United and British Airways first. You only need to search United to learn what awards are available in the Star Alliance, which includes Air Canada and Lufthansa. Likewise, you can find OneWorld Alliance awards with British Airways so you don't have to duplicate your search with other OneWorld partners such as Iberia and Aer Lingus. Searching the Flying Blue (the frequent flier program of Air France and KLM) will help you find award travel options with SkyTeam Alliance. While this can save time, you will need to create logins with the airlines that you want to search and plan to hunt around a bit for the award seats you want, at the lowest mileage levels.

Award search tools can be lifesavers. Thankfully, there's some award search tools out there that can automate this process, including Point.me and Seats.aero. These pay apps will search multiple programs at once, but you still may need to do many searches to find the awards you want on the days you want. When you locate a really good award, your best bet is to book it as soon as possible. Award seats constantly appear and disappear and quickly locking in the cornerstone of your trip is essential. There's just been too many times that I've contemplated pulling the trigger for a few days, only to find that it's not available when I've gone back to try and book it.

Tips for making international free travel booking a bit easier. As I work through this process, one of the things I do to help arrange

reward travel to Europe is to begin my award trip at an international gateway airport and obtain a "positioning flight" to get there. For me, living in Denver, I often book my award portion of the trip to Europe starting from New York, LA, or Chicago because adding the flight from Denver to those gateway destinations can often double the price of the award. So, it's much cheaper for me to use an award flight on Southwest, or another airline, as a positioning flight to get me to the gateway airport where my European award trip starts. And while that can add extra time to my travel, I usually look on the bright side and just enjoy the stopover and take an extra day in those U.S. gateway cities.

When I need the flexibility, I'll often book an award flight to a European gateway rather than to my intended final destination. For example, on our family's most recent trip to Europe we planned a vacation in Greece but flew to London first. We spent two days and one night seeing the city before continuing on to Greece. To get there from London, we simply purchased tickets for less than $100 each on EasyJet, one of Europe's many ultra-discount carriers. In Europe, airlines like EasyJet, Ryanair, Wizz Air, and Vueling will often sell tickets for under $100, making this an irresistible way to reposition yourself around the continent. Just be aware that these airlines have a business model that forces you to pay for extras like carry-on bags, checked bags, and seat assignments. But even when you factor in these costs, this can be a very affordable way to get around Europe, especially if you're willing to travel light. It's also a good idea to consider train travel within Europe, which has a network of high-speed lines that are more affordable and comfortable than what Americans are used to.

Step 2: Book hotel awards for Europe

As with flights, booking a hotel award in Europe is a little more challenging than doing so domestically. Sure, there are some reasonably priced Hyatts in Europe, but there aren't nearly as many as you'll find in the U.S. And often, the Hyatt and Hilton hotels that you find in Europe will be luxury properties that will cost tens of thousands of points per night, even though with Marriott, you may have better luck finding reasonably priced awards.

So, when booking hotels in Europe, it can help to look at some alternative programs. In the U.S., Choice Hotels is largely known for budget properties such as EconoLodge, Comfort Inn, and Clarion brands. But in parts of Europe, Choice hotels can be higher quality than what you typically find in the U.S., as well as being a bargain. For example, it's not uncommon to find excellent Choice hotels located in historic buildings in Europe, available for 10,000 to 20,000 Choice points per night. As I mentioned previously, the Comfort Hotel Bolivar in Rome, for instance, is a charming property in a quiet courtyard in the middle of the city. A room with three single beds can cost just 16,000 points in the Choice privileges program.

You can transfer American Express Membership Rewards points or Capital One Miles to the Choice Privileges program at a 1 to 1 ratio. But you can do much better by transferring Citi ThankYou Points, or points from the new Wells Fargo Autograph Journey card to Choice at a 1 to 2 ratio. That means for merely 8,000 Citi points, you can book a hotel in Rome that costs $750, which is a fantastic value at over nine cents in value per point redeemed.

Step 3: Transfer the points.

Transferring your reward points from a program like Chase Ultimate Rewards or American Express Membership Rewards is pretty quick and easy. As always, you want to make sure that you find the available award space first, and only then transfer your rewards to points or miles. Immediately book your reservations as soon as the points are transferred.

Step 4: Finish planning your trip.

Once you have your flights and hotels booked, it's time to fill in the remaining pieces. This could be airport transfers, trains, or flights between cities in Europe or car rentals (it's best to avoid renting a car in major European cities due to the high cost and low availability of parking). You'll also want to book tickets to major tourist attractions, as these can sell out during peak periods.

RECIPE 3: TRIP TO HAWAII

For many Americans, Hawaii is the ultimate domestic destination. It's exotic, with its own distinct food, culture, and music. And while you have to go halfway across an ocean to get there, you don't need to carry a passport or exchange currency.

But as anyone who has ever visited Hawaii can tell you, it's expensive — that is unless you travel there using the points and miles you have amassed using the tips and tricks I've outlined in this book. I paid nearly nothing for our flights and lodging on the most recent trip our family took to Hawaii.

Here's how to do it:

Ingredients:

1. Turkish Airlines Miles & Smiles points. These can be transferred from Citi ThankYou Points, Bilt Rewards, or Capital One Miles. Southwest points also works well if you have a Companion Pass.
2. Hotel points (these can be with any of the major programs, but unfortunately, you'll need a lot of them).

HOW TO PREPARE:

Step 1: Book your flight.

Why would you book a ticket to Hawaii using Turkish Airlines miles? Will you have to change planes in Istanbul to get there? Of course not. Not only is Turkish Airlines a member of the Star Alliance, but it offers one-way economy class tickets to Hawaii on its partner, United Airlines, for a mere 10,000 miles each. Compare this to the 22,500 miles charged by United for the exact same flights, and you'll be excited to transfer your Citi ThankYou Points or Capital One Miles to Turkish miles.

What's the catch? You'll need to find United Airlines award availability at their lowest mileage levels. To do this, go to United. com and begin searching for flights. You'll usually have to look very far in advance, ideally 11 months out, when the flights become available for booking. The award flights that you find on its Star Alliance partners should be available as awards from any of its partners, such as Air Canada, Avianca, or Turkish. United's website works great for finding flights on its Star Alliance partners, but just note that it will show you more award flights operated

by United that are available when you try to use miles from its partners.

Booking United flights through Turkish isn't hard, but you'll be frustrated if you don't know a few tricks. First, look for flights on United.com at the lowest mileage levels. Then, after creating a free account with Turkish, make sure to navigate to their Star Alliance award search tool. Do this by clicking on your name in the top-right corner, then choosing the option for "Miles Transactions." On the next screen, select the option for Star Alliance award tickets, and then click "Book now."

Sometimes you might not find the flights you see on United. com available on Turkish Airlines' website. In this case, you may have to call Turkish Airlines and ask them to look for the flights you found at United.com, one at a time. Another option is to email one of their offices, which will hold the award while you transfer the miles and fill out some paperwork.

For those of you who don't want to try to use Turkish Miles to fly United, Southwest points can work very well. And if you have their Companion Pass, you're basically buying one ticket with points and getting the other free.

Step 2: Book accommodations.

There are several hotel programs that work well for booking vacation stays in Hawaii, but the cost in points can be high. One exception is Wyndham points, which are fantastic for booking vacation rentals through Vacasa.com. In addition to there being quite a few of these types of vacation homes and condos to rent, some of these properties can be reserved for just 15,000 points per bedroom, per night for rentals less than $250-per-night. Unfortunately, most properties in Hawaii cost more, and Wyndham will charge 30,000 points per night, per bedroom for rentals between $250 to $500 per night. Thankfully, if you're a Wyndham Earner credit card holder, you get a 10 percent discount on your booking, bringing the price down to just 13,500 or 27,000 points per bedroom, per night. That means that a seven-night-stay could cost as little as 94,500 points but will likely be as much as 189,000. Fortunately, Wyndham points are pretty easy to earn, as the Wyndham Business Earner card offers 5x points for utilities and an incredible 8x on gas. You can also earn Wyndham points through their business and personal credit cards, or by transferring them from the Citi ThankYou Points program.

To find awards, look at Vacasa.com, the vacation rental management company that Wyndham acquired. Be careful to limit the number of bedrooms you are looking for as that will determine the price. Once you find availability for the room that you want, call 800-441-1034 to book it with your Wyndham Rewards points. On our last trip to Hawaii, I booked a condo in Maui on Kaanapali Beach this way, with a spectacular view of the ocean. One of the highlights of the trip was being able to spot whales, right from our condo. It was also nice to have a kitchen and a washer/dryer. Having the kitchen allowed us to save time and money by avoiding the need to eat out every meal. And with the washer/dryer, we didn't have to bring along 10 days-worth of clothing.

Another great option for Hawaii is Hilton points, as their Hilton Honors program will give you a fifth night free when you book a five-night stay, and won't add any dreaded "resort fees" to your

award stay. Marriott also gives you a fifth night free but leaves you on the hook for resort fees. Hyatt can be a great option as it waives resort fees and even parking charges for award stays. However, their properties in Hawaii tend to be very pricey, so expect to pay at least 25,000 points a night, and there is no fifth-night free offer.

Step 3: Transferring the points.

As with the other recipes, always find the awards first, then transfer the points you need to book them. Once the points show up in your airline or hotel account, you should immediately book your awards, before they disappear.

Step 4: Finish planning your trip.

Fill in the rest of the details of your trip. I'd start with a rental car, as one is usually necessary in Hawaii. You might also want to make dinner reservations, as they can be scarce at some of the more popular restaurants.

CONCLUSION

Between business trips, family vacations and visiting relatives, I book a lot of award trips. But just like anyone who gets better and faster at cooking their favorite dishes the more they practice, I find myself spending less time planning trips than I used to. These three recipes can't cover every possible trip you'll take, but they're a great start. And by the time that you've successfully cooked up these "recipes," you'll be ready to tackle some even greater award travel challenges.

CHAPTER 7 CHALLENGE:

1. Where do you want to travel to next? It's best to start your award travel journey with modest goals.

2. What airlines will best serve you on your trip? Which hotels there are available for points and miles?

3. What credit cards offer you the points and miles needed to book this trip for free? Remember to include not just cards co-branded with the airline or hotel, but also flexible travel rewards cards that offer points that can be transferred to these airline and hotel programs.

CHAPTER 8:
Advanced Tips and Tricks

By now, you should understand the basics of award travel and all the many ways to take advantage of it. In this final chapter, I'd like to take your award travel knowledge to the next level by sharing some of the more advanced techniques I've learned over the years.

SOUTHWEST COMPANION PASS

While there are a few airline credit cards that offer a one-time companion certificate, Southwest Airlines, in my opinion, offers the best type of pass out there because it can be used to add a designated traveler to an *unlimited* number of tickets. I have hailed the many wonderful features of the Southwest Companion Pass in previous chapters and want to encourage you to take advantage of it if it makes sense for you and your family.

To qualify for your Companion Pass, you must earn 135,000 Southwest Rapid Rewards points (125,000 for holders of a Southwest Rapid Rewards credit card from Chase) or take 100 one-way flights in a calendar year. I love to fly, but not that much! Thankfully, you can easily qualify for the Companion Pass just by signing up for two credit cards. While the offers fluctuate every few months, you can usually earn the Companion Pass by receiving the sign-up bonuses for one personal and one small business Southwest credit card from Chase. As of this writing, the Southwest Rapid Rewards personal cards are offering new applicants 50,000 points after spending just $1,000 within three months, and the Rapid Rewards Performance small business card is offering 80,000 points after spending $5,000 within three months. These are pretty typical offers, but sometimes there are even better ones available as well. I always feature the best offers on my website: jasonsteele.com/cards.

So, imagine you apply for both cards and spend the total of $6,000 to receive both bonuses. You'll end up with at least 141,000 Rapid Rewards points, which is more than enough to receive the Companion Pass. And what many people don't realize is that you don'tactually have to redeem those points to get the pass, you simply have to earn them. This means that you receive a Companion Pass and you still get to spend the 141,000 points on award travel! Since Southwest points are worth about 1.4 cents each towards award tickets, you're looking at about $2,000 worth of airline tickets. Add in your companion, and now you're talking about nearly $4,000 of travel. You'll incur $200 to $300 in fees, but that's pennies on the dollar compared to the free travel that you can earn. It's a fabulous deal in my opinion and one of the best ways I use points and miles to travel for free.

Be aware that timing is key to making this deal work best. I like to sign up for the cards at the end of the year, making sure

not to spend enough to receive my sign-up bonus until I'm in the statement period that ends in January. That way I earn the bonus points in January and receive a Companion Pass that's valid until December 31st of the following year. That means that I get nearly two years of use from the pass. In fact, I'll request that my payment due date be the 26th of the month so that my statement closes on the 1st. I meet my minimum spending requirement in December, and the points are awarded to me on or about January 1. Typically, I'll keep the account open for a year (as you always should, see Chapter 6) and close it after the annual fee comes due. A year later, I'll sign up for the card again. For over 10 years, my wife and I have both used this strategy to continuously hold Companion Passes.

Southwest requires that you designate a specific traveling companion for the pass, and I usually choose one of my children as my companion, but Southwest allows you to change companions up to three times per year. This allows me to switch children, or even change my companion to my wife if we're lucky enough to travel together without the kids.

Now, you may be wondering if my family is taking advantage of Southwest by doing this. Do they hate us? Not at all. Southwest changed the terms of their credit cards a few years ago to be explicit about the signup bonus from the Rapid Rewards credit cards qualified towards the Companion Pass.

THE TRICK TO FINDING EXTRA UNITED AWARD SPACE

Here's a simple but valuable trick that will help you get the most value from the United MileagePlus frequent flier program. United, like most airlines, is very stingy with the number of award seats that it offers at the lowest mileage levels — the so-called "Saver" awards. But it turns out that United will offer additional Saver awards to those who hold elite status in the program, as well as anyone who has a United MileagePlus credit card from Chase.

So, if you earn United MileagePlus miles, or like to transfer your Chase Ultimate Rewards points to United, then I strongly recommend you get a United Mileage Plus card from Chase. These cards will offer a generous sign-up bonus and allow you to book economy class award flights for the lowest mileage amounts. And after you've had the card for a year, you don't have to keep paying the annual fee. Instead, you can ask to downgrade to the United Gateway card, a version that doesn't have an annual fee.

MEETING THE REQUIREMENTS FOR SPENDING AND SIGNUP BONUSES

One of the issues that I face in signing up for three or four new cards each year is finding ways to meet the minimum spending requirements to earn all of these bonuses. Sometimes, award travel enthusiasts will call this "meeting spend." Thankfully, I know several ways to meet spend efficiently.

SPEND SHIFTING

First, consider a strategy I think of as "spend shifting." This is when you make payments now for things you would usually pay for later. For example, you can use your card to pay large bills like insurance or utilities *early*. You can also purchase a gift card that you'll use later. This could either be a merchant gift card for a place that you shop regularly, or it could be a generic card that works at any store that accepts Visa or Mastercard.

PAY TAXES WITH A CREDIT CARD

Another option is to pay your taxes with a credit card. When you use a card to pay federal income taxes, you'll incur fees of between 1.82 and 1.98 percent, and normally I would say . this isn't worth the cost, especially when you will usually only earn one or two points per dollar spent with the credit card you use. But if you need to spend $10,000 to earn a signup bonus of 100,000 points, then it's like earning 11x points per dollar spent. That's easily worth paying up to 2 percent extra in fees on your tax bill, especially when you consider that numerous merchants, utility companies, and contractors now add fees of around 3 percent for the privilege of paying with a credit card for their products and services. You're already incurring fees, for instance, to use a card to pay for school tuition, home improvements, and municipal utilities. Why not pay the even lower user-fee incurred by the IRS to pay your taxes with a credit card?

PAY EVERYONE ELSE'S BILL AT DINNER

Another way to "meet spend" is by paying the restaurant bills for friends and family members when you go out to eat. You can be sure that every time I go to dinner with a group of friends, I'll offer to pay the bill with my credit card. If you know people who don't use credit cards or aren't into credit card rewards, just ask them if you can pay their bills and then have them reimburse you with cash or electronic transfers.

BOOKING AWARD TRAVEL FOR LARGE GROUPS

I absolutely love traveling with my family, and all of my children have been on airplanes starting around three months of age, but booking award travel for five or more people can be challenging. As much as I love reading award travel blogs written by singles and couples extolling the virtues of getting away for free, I'm not sure many of them understand how difficult it can be to arrange award travel for larger groups. But since I also love a challenge, I've made it my mission to seek out every possible strategy and loophole to get my family to where we need to go with award tickets, and often in business class, and I want to share some of these strategies with you here.

BOOK IN ADVANCE

First, you will always want to book award tickets as far in advance as possible. I emphasized the importance of this in my "Europe trip recipe" in Chapter 7, and as far as groups are concerned, it applies for any destination, not just international flights. Sure, some airlines will release unsold seats as additional award space as you get closer to the date of the flight, but that's not predictable. However, you can count on most airlines releasing most of their available award seats (at the lowest mileage levels) about 11 months out. This is also when they begin selling seats for cash. And since most people traveling in large groups are doing so with school-age children and must work around the inflexibility of their kid's school schedule, booking in advance just makes sense. Since school schedules are usually published one or two years in advance, you should have no problem planning major vacations at least 11 months ahead of your intended travel dates.

Of course, booking your trips 11 months out kills any chance you had of being spontaneous, but it also has several advantages beyond just finding award availability at the lowest mileage levels.

For example, because you booked so far ahead, it is likely that flight times and airline schedules will change as you get closer to your travel dates. When that happens you can use this potential inconvenience to request that the airline resolve the change in your favor by giving you more favorable flights. For example, if you book tickets on United from Denver to London, via Newark, and one of the flights changes, then you could ask that you be accommodated on one of their non-stop flights.

"SPLIT THE TEAM"

When booking a group of five or more, you'll have no problem with airlines like Southwest, Delta and JetBlue — which open up every unsold seat as an award — as their points are closely tied to the cash price of a ticket. But when traveling overseas, Southwest and JetBlue won't be of much help (although JetBlue now flies to a few European destinations), and you'll rarely find five or more of the lowest priced award seats on the same flight. This is especially true when you have the desire, and the miles, to fly in business class.

So, to resolve this problem, my family will agree to "split the team" on some occasions. This is when two of us are on one flight and three of us are on another. It doesn't seem ideal, but we've found that sometimes it's actually easiest to travel in two small groups rather than one large one.

FINDING ELUSIVE AWARD SPACE

Even when you're not traveling with a large group, you can still have trouble finding the award seats you need at the lowest mileage levels. Again, this is harder when you're looking for international business class awards.

If you're not finding the award seats you want at the lowest mileage levels, then you need to get creative. As I've mentioned before, I'm a big fan of positioning flights that allow us to fly to or from a gateway city, and perhaps spend a day or two there before continuing to our final destination.

I also believe in using award search tools like Point.me and Seats.aero to search for bargain-priced awards across multiple frequent flier programs that I have access to through credit cards that offer flexible travel rewards points.

If it's proving to be too difficult to find award flights and you're about to give up, feel free to reach out to your fellow award travel enthusiasts on sites like FlyerTalk.com, which is an online forum. They may have ideas and tips for you that you had not previously considered. And when you simply don't have the time or energy to do the research, you can hire an award travel booking service to help you or a coach, such as myself. Helping clients learn about the more advanced tips and tools for booking award travel that I know about is something I've done for my clients in the past and I like to tell them I'll help them save thousands of dollars for a reasonable fee.

INFANT AWARD TRAVEL

Some travelers will bristle at the notion of taking an infant on an airplane, but my wife and I have had many successful flights with our children as infants. And while some will cite crying babies as a reason not to travel with an infant, I've had enough negative expe-

riences with disruptive adults to know that humans of every age are equally capable of bad behavior.

When traveling within the United States, infants under two years of age can travel on the lap of an adult for no extra charge. Southwest has an unusual habit of demanding proof of age before accepting an infant and falsely claiming that they are required to document the child's age (the FAA has no such documentation requirement). That leaves parents forced to provide an original or photocopy of the child's birth certificate, passport, or immunization record, even when they're traveling with a baby that's obviously nowhere close to two years old.

In our experience, traveling with a lap child works well for children under 18 months and on shorter flights. There's also plenty of space in business or first class. But when you start traveling on longer flights, and when the child gets closer to age two, it's far more practical to purchase a seat for your infant.

When using frequent flier miles to travel internationally, most airlines will charge a lap child fee of 10 percent of the cash price of a ticket. This is where it gets tricky as there's nothing to document if it's 10 percent of a discounted fare or a full-fare ticket. Ten percent doesn't sound like much, but I've been asked to pay $800 to carry my child on my lap in business class! Thankfully there are a few airlines that allow you to add a lap child to an award ticket for just 10 percent of the miles required, or less. These include All Nippon Airways (ANA) and British Airways that charge only 10 percent of the miles. Emirates will charge 10 percent of the miles for economy class but 10 percent of the fare in dollars for business and first-class awards. Virgin Atlantic prices awards for 1,000 miles in economy, each way, 2,000 in premium economy, and 5,000 in Upper Class (their version of business class). Air Canada charges only $25 Canadian dollars or 2,500 miles.

RENTAL CAR TRICKS

Once you've booked your airfare and hotel, preferably with points and miles, one of the biggest remaining expenses will often be car rental. Rental prices have soared since COVID subsided because companies had to sell off much of their fleets to avoid bankruptcy during the crisis, only to find supply chain shortages limited their ability to acquire new vehicles.

USE DISCOUNT CODES

To find the best deal on a rental car in the aftermath of COVID, I suggest using a discount code that offers you a negotiated rate. These codes are often available to employees of large companies, universities, and government organizations. You can also access codes offered to college alumni and to members of groups such as sports associations, AAA, and AARP. You might find that there are many codes you can use; finding the best ones is often through trial and error.

JOIN FREQUENT RENTER PROGRAMS

You also want to make sure to join the rental car company's frequent renter program, which will allow you to skip the counter and go straight to your car. If you have a Chase Sapphire Reserve or American Express Platinum, then you get access to elite programs with Hertz and National.

Several rental car companies now let you choose your own car, a practice introduced by National. In fact, National remains my

favorite program as it has a simple, yet valuable rewards program that gives you a free day after renting just a few times (the number depends on your status level in the program). National will also match your status with other rental companies, and even airline and hotel programs.

USE YOUR CARD FOR RENTAL CAR INSURANCE

Another way to save money is to rely on your credit card for rental car insurance. This allows you to decline the expensive, optional insurance that's aggressively sold at the counter. I like the Chase Sapphire Reserve and Sapphire Preferred, which offer primary rental car insurance. Unlike many credit cards that only extend secondary coverage, having primary means that you don't have to file a claim with your personal vehicle policy.

I'm also a big fan of the American Express Premium Rental Car Coverage option. For a fee of about $20 to $25, per rental, you get primary coverage that even applies to luxury cars. Since the cost is per rental, and not per day, this is ideal for longer rentals and is a no-brainer when you rent a car in a developing country where damage seems much more likely. Just keep in mind that coverage doesn't apply in Australia, Ireland, Israel, Italy, Jamaica, and New Zealand. This seems very random, but it has to do with each of these countries' unusual liability insurance requirements.

AIRPORT SECURITY

USE TSA PRE-CHECK

Perhaps the biggest pain point in airline travel is having to stand in line and go through invasive TSA security. Yet most frequent travelers know that you can avoid the worst parts of security and most of the lines if you're a member of the TSA PreCheck program. For those who remember what traveling was like before the September 11attacks, you can think of PreCheck as essentially pre-9/11 security. Getting approved to use this program means that you keep your shoes, belts, and light jackets on; you keep your liquids and laptops in your suitcase; and you pass through a simple metal detector instead of a full body scanner. And children 12 and under can use the TSA PreCheck lines when traveling with an adult member of PreCheck.

At the time of this writing, a five-year membership in the TSA PreCheck program is available for just $78. This is already a bargain, but thankfully, many travel rewards credit cards now include a $100 credit towards the application fees for TSA PreCheck (or Global Entry, which includes TSA PreCheck). These cards include the Chase Sapphire Reserve, Capital One Venture and Venture X, American Express Platinum, United Explorer, and many others.

GLOBAL ENTRY PROGRAM

The Global Entry program allows you to skip the lines at immigration when traveling to the U.S. It has a $120 application fee and it also includes TSA PreCheck. Unfortunately, it can be a big hassle to get it. First, you must fill out a very long form online. Then you are required to schedule an appointment for an interview and fingerprints at an international airport, and often the schedule is booked solid for months. Once you have an appointment, you must go to the airport to finish the enrollment process before you can use this service. And there's always a chance that you may

have to visit the airport again to renew it. But once you have it, you can speed through the passport controls when you arrive, potentially saving hours in line. Just note that all passengers must be enrolled in Global Entry, even infants.

CLEAR

Another option that helps streamline airport security checks is called CLEAR. This is a private identity verification service that can be used in conjunction with PreCheck, and theoretically is supposed to be even faster than PreCheck alone. Instead of presenting ID to the TSA , CLEAR members can have their eyes or fingerprints scanned by a kiosk at participating airports. Sometimes this results in being able to skip the PreCheck lines altogether and head right to the front. There is one problem, however, that I'm starting to see with CLEAR since COVID, and that's lines as long for CLEAR as they are for PreCheck, and sometimes even longer.

To use CLEAR, you must pay an annual membership of $199, but keep in mind that the CLEAR service is not yet available in all airports across the world. There are discounts available for those who are members of United or Delta's frequent flier programs or for adding additional family members. CLEAR credits are also offered by the American Express Platinum and Green cards.

LOUNGE ACCESS

One of the perks that really separates award travel enthusiasts from the average traveler is their love of lounges. After breezing through security with PreCheck and CLEAR, I'll typically head straight to a lounge where I'll hole up until just before boarding begins.

BASIC LOUNGES

There are several kinds of airport lounges which range from spartan to luxurious. The most basic lounges will often include snacks, places to work, and free Wi-Fi and are usually part of the Priority Pass program, which is frequently included as a credit card benefit. Credit cards that have this benefit include the Chase Sapphire Reserve, American Express Platinum, and Capital One Venture X. While there are well over 1,000 basic-type lounges available throughout the world, relatively few of them are in the United States. In contrast, you'll find a Priority Pass lounge in nearly every international airport around the world, and several locations at some of the larger ones.

AIRLINE LOUNGES

Airlines also have their own lounges, which are offered to travelers who are flying international business class, those who have a premium airline credit card, and those with top-tier elite status. You can also gain access to such lounges by purchasing a membership or a day pass for around $50. These lounges tend to be a little nicer than the Priority Pass lounges, and some, like United Polaris, are quite deluxe. They will often include plentiful seating, showers, a buffet and bar, and even finer dining.

Some airlines have very special lounges just for their international first-class customers. For example, Lufthansa has a first-class lounge in Frankfurt that is technically its own terminal with exclusive security screening. There, you can order fine dining from a complimentary menu before being driven to your aircraft in a Mercedes. There are only a few of these lounges available

throughout the world, but if you get a chance to visit one, I highly recommend it.

American Express has a network of Centurion lounges that offer an experience that's somewhere between a business-class and first-class airline lounge. You can enjoy some pretty good food from their buffet, a well-stocked bar, and very comfortable seating. Access is available for American Express Platinum cardholders, but you can't let any guests in unless you complete $75,000 of spending in a calendar year. Capital One is also building a network of lounges, but only three have been announced in Denver, Washington-Dulles, and Dallas-Fort Worth airports. Chase is also opening up its own Sapphire Lounges for those who hold its Sapphire Reserve card.

AWARD TRAVEL SWEET SPOTS

If you spend even a little time looking at all of the ways to redeem your points and miles, you'll quickly realize that most of the options offer very poor value. For example, it's almost never a good idea to redeem your travel rewards points or miles for things like merchandise or gift cards, which will typically extend just a penny in value per point or mile redeemed, and sometimes not even that much. As I have emphasized in other chapters, the best redemption values will often come from booking business-class international airline awards at the lowest mileage levels. You can also receive excellent value from hotel awards, which are much more easily available. When you find these awards and are able to book them, you can often receive several cents in value per point or mile redeemed. These opportunities are often referred to as "sweet spots," and in this section I will share my list of favorites. Just keep in mind that this list is only accurate at the time of publishing, and it's always possible that some of these won't be available at the time you read this. In fact, they will all disappear eventually, but new ones will always arise. For a current list, visit my website at jasonsteele.com.

1. ANA BUSINESS CLASS TO EUROPE, THE MIDDLE EAST, AND AFRICA

ANA is All Nippon Airways of Japan, and it's had one of the most generous business- class award charts for a long time. Award flights from North America to Europe are just 100,000 miles, round-trip, in business class. Africa and the Middle East aren't much higher at 130,000 miles. Of course, you don't have to fly there via Japan, as ANA is a member of the Star Alliance, which includes 25 other airlines, 15 of which are in North America, Europe, and Africa.

The good news is that ANA is a transfer partner of the American Express Membership Rewards program, so their miles are fairly easy to acquire. And there are plenty of options to get you to your destination for these incredibly low prices. I've personally used ANA miles to book numerous flights for family, friends, and myself to Europe and Africa. The bad news, however, is that ANA will impose massive fuel surcharges for flights on many of these carriers, so you need to pay attention to that when booking the flight. For example, I once priced a Swiss Airlines flight through ANA from New York to Geneva that added over $1,000 to the reservation; and that's per-person, one way! To avoid these surcharges, focus on ANA's airline partners that have low or no additional charges like Ethiopian, Asiana, LOT Polish, Thai,

Turkish, and United. Avoid Austrian, Swiss, and Lufthansa, or just rationalize spending about the price of an economy class ticket and your miles in order to enjoy business class. You should always be aware that you can only book these tickets as a round-trip; ANA doesn't offer one-way partner awards.

2. TURKISH AIRLINES FLIGHTS WITHIN THE UNITED STATES (INCLUDING ALASKA, HAWAII AND PUERTO RICO).

Turkish Airlines is another Star Alliance partner that has a few very well-priced award options. For 10,000 miles, you can book a one-way economy class flight within the United States, Alaska, Hawaii, and Puerto Rico.

That said, United is the only Star Alliance carrier in the U.S., so it's your only option. Furthermore, United can be very stingy with award space offered to its partners (it's much more generous when you book using United miles, and you have a United credit card or elite status with United). In fact, first-class tickets can theoretically be booked for just 12,500 miles each way, but it's extremely rare to find those. However, if you search for awards very far into the future, United can sometimes offer several award seats on the same flight. To search for award space, use United. com, and don't login to make sure you're seeing the award space available to partners at their lowest mileage levels.

For example, awards to Hawaii that appear at 22,500 miles each way on United's website will be bookable with just 10.000 Turkish Miles. Once you find the space you're looking for, verify that the Turkish Airlines website also shows it. But even if it doesn't appear, you may still be able to book it by contacting a Turkish Airlines reservation office in the U.S. In fact, you'll have to do so if you are booking an award that includes other people. You can hold the award while you complete required paperwork, but it's all worth it if you can snag an ultra-low-priced award to Hawaii. You can get Turkish Airlines miles by transferring points from the Citi ThankYou rewards program, or from Capital One Miles.

3. ANA PREMIUM AWARDS USING VIRGIN ATLANTIC MILES

As is often the case, you'll find the best deal when you book award flights operated by an airline's partner, as carriers tend to charge more miles for awards on their own flights. So just as ANA offers very low-priced awards on its partners, the best deals for ANA flights are offered by another airline. For ANA flights from the west coast, Virgin Atlantic charges a mere52,500 miles each way in business class, and 72,500 miles for awards in its ultra-luxurious international first class. From the east coast, the prices are only slightly higher at 60,000 for business and 85,000 for first. Expect to pay some relatively minor fuel surcharges.

4. SHORT-HAUL AWARDS WITH UNITED MILES

While it's not really distance-based, United's MileagePlus frequent flier program offers discounted awards on flights of less than 800 miles within the same region. Often these short flights can be very expensive, especially when booked without much advance notice. But fortunately, these award prices are available when you book flights operated by United, its Star Alliance partners, and even its non-Alliance partners. You can transfer your Chase Ultimate Rewards points to United. Chase also offers numerous credit cards co-branded with United.

CONCLUSION

You've made it! You've finished an entire book on how to travel for free, and now the world is your oyster! That's because you're now prepared to take advantage of some pretty exciting opportunities to travel anywhere on Earth, in style, for little to no cost. Of course, grasping all the nuances of award travel is a big task, but it's one that I hope I have shown you can not only be fun, but also deliver a huge payout.

For some, this book has lit a fire in you to learn everything you possibly can on the subject. Like me, you may find that you now have a keen interest in seeking out and absorbing all the information available on reward travel. If that sounds like you, I urge you to peruse the many websites and online forums that are always offering the latest news on award travel. Better yet, I encourage you to attend the numerous events where award travel enthusiasts meet to share their experiences, insights, and even a few secret techniques. I'm proud to have been featured as a speaker at many of these events.

For other readers who aren't totally ready to plunge themselves completely into the subject, it is my hope that this book has at least whet your appetite and given you the desire to try some of the techniques I have outlined. Maybe you're the kind of person that would rather just dine at a five-star restaurant than become the gourmet who cooks all the amazing culinary delights for that restaurant. If that sounds like you, then I'm happy to offer a couple of options that will help you take advantage of award travel without having to immerse yourself into every aspect of it:

First, I offer award travel consultations. I really enjoy working directly with people to help them find a strategy that best fits their needs. These consultations start with an inventory of all of your household and small business credit cards, along with your balances of travel rewards earned from airlines and hotel programs. We then discuss your award travel goals and develop a strategy to reach them. The consultation concludes with a written set of specific, personalized recommendations. It typically lasts about two hours and can be done in person, over the phone, or through a video conference. I've done many of these coaching sessions, and I've never failed to help my clients realize thousands of dollars of award travel. I also offer a list of the latest credit card offers, along with my reviews of them at my website, JasonSteele.com.

No matter how little or how much you get involved with the things you have learned in this book, remember that award travel is about more than just saving money, it's about literally opening yourself up to a world of new possibilities. As I noted at the beginning of the book, there's something about visiting a place that will forever connect you with the land and its people. For some, award travel will be about sightseeing in major cities and taking guided tours. Others will use their points and miles to experience adventures in the most remote corners of the Earth. Wherever you've dreamed of going, I hope that you can use this book to help you get there.

While it's impossible to document every tip and trick out there, I've hopefully helped you build a solid foundation from which to start earning and redeeming rewards towards free travel. I encourage you to get excited about identifying and utilizing new credit cards, taking advantage of exciting promotions, and applying innovative ways to redeem points. With each successful award trip you plan and take, you'll be energized towards finding the next big opportunity, allowing you to travel further, and in greater luxury than you may have ever imagined. And when you're visiting the lounge, or settling into business class for a long-haul flight, take a look around. I might just be sitting there next to you.

Happy travels!

RECOMMENDED AWARD
TRAVEL RESOURCES

JasonSteele.com: This is my personal website that includes several travel resources. From here, you can reach out to me and schedule an award travel consultation, and find links to the latest credit card reviews and offers. I also have a list of the outlets I've contributed to and links to my work there.

AwardWallet.com: A free tool that helps you track and organize your points and miles. It also stores your passwords and automates your logins.

BoardingArea.com: A collection of travel rewards websites from around the world — my favorites include: "View from the Wing," "One Mile at a Time," "Miles to Memories," "Live and Let Fly," and "Frequent Miler."

DansDeals.com: Website offering many kinds of consumer deals, but mainly specializes in award travel opportunities.

FlyerTalk.com: Public forum for travelers to share travel experiences, tips, and tricks.

Masking Tape: Put a small strip on top of the credit cards in your wallet and label them "Gas," "Groceries," "Dining," or Non-bonus Spending" to remind you what each card is best used for.

ThePointsGuy.com: This is the largest and most popular website for those seeking to earn and spend travel rewards.

Travel Freely: An app that helps you track your credit cards and travel rewards.

TPG App: Helps you improve your spending habits, maximize rewards, and track your progress.

NOTES

INTRODUCTION

U.S. State Department. Only 44.4 percent of Americans have a passport. https://travel.state.gov/content/dam/travel/CA-By-the-Number-2020.pdf

Mark Twain, The Innocents at Home, (London: Chatto&Windus, 1906). "Travel is fatal to prejudice, bigotry, and narrow-mindedness, and many of our people need it sorely on these accounts."

Becky Pokora, Dylan Pearl,"2024 vs. 2023 Travel Trends: 40% of Americans Plan to Travel More this Year," *Forbes Advisor,*(January 2024) https://www.forbes.com/advisor/credit-cards/travel-rewards/survey-travel-plans2024/#:~:text=Key%20Takeaways,Americans%20took%20an&text=92%25%20of%20travelers%20expect%20to,to%20our%202023%20survey%20findings.

CHAPTER 1

Poonkulali Thangavelu, "More Cardholders Carrying Balances, Credit Card Debt," *Bankrate.com*, (January 8, 2024), https://www.bankrate.com/finance/credit-cards/credit-card-debt-survey/. \

Federal Reserve Bank, report on consumer credit as of May 2023, https://www.federalreserve.gov/releases/g19/current/.

CHAPTER 2

Index by Pinger, "Small Business, Side Hustle, and Freelance Insights Survey," (October 30, 2023), https://getindex.com/resources/small-business-side-hustle-survey-fall-2023. "Sixty-seven percent of Americans have a small business or perform freelance work, often called a 'side hustle.'Another 17 percent plan to start a small business, side hustle, or begin accepting freelance work."

CHAPTER 3

BenjiStawski and Ben Smithson, "JetBlue TrueBlue Program: Earn and Redeem Points, Transfer Partners, and More," *ThePointsGuy.com*, (March 22, 2024),https://thepointsguy.com/guide/jetblue-trueblue-program/. "You can expect a fairly consistent 1.3 cents of value per TrueBlue point. Based on our experiences, the redemption value tends to be slightly lower for JetBlue Mint award tickets."

Kimberly Palmer, Erin Hurd, Sally French, "The Guide to JetBlue TrueBlue," *Nerdwallet.com*, (April 29, 2024),https://www.nerdwallet.com/article/travel/jetblue-trueblue-rewards-program-the-complete-guide. "Because JetBlue points are typically "fixed" to the value of cash prices, it's harder to find sweet spots. You won't usually get outsized value for your TrueBlue points, but rest assured that you'll generally get at least 1 cent per point value at minimum."

CHAPTER 4

Anya Kartashova, "Four Reasons to Skip Marriott Bonvoy," *NerdWallet,* (September 7, 2023), https://www.nerdwallet.com/article/travel/reasons-to-skip-marriott-bonvoy.

CHAPTER 6

Dreamworks Pictures, The Montecito Picture Company, *Up in the Air,* (2009); Ryan Bingham character states: "I don't spend a nickel, if I can help it, unless it somehow profits my mileage account."

ABOUT THE AUTHOR

Jason Steele is one of America's leading experts on credit cards and travel rewards. Since 2008, he has contributed to over 100 outlets including *Forbes*, *USA Today*, *Time*, *Newsweek*, and the *Wall Street Journal*.

In 2012, Jason was asked to be the first contributor to ThePointsGuy.com, one of the most popular websites about credit cards and travel rewards. He is also the founder and producer of CardCon: The Conference for Credit Card Media; and the founder of The Steele Team, LLC, which offers consulting services for individuals, small business owners, and corporations in the credit card industry.

Jason lives in Denver, Colorado with his wife Janna and their three children. He holds a commercial pilot's license and is a Certified Flight Instructor (CFI). He enjoys cycling, snowboarding and wilderness camping. You can reach Jason via his website: JasonSteele.com

Want to connect with Jason Steele and explore more about his work?

Scan the QR code below to access exclusive content, updates, and insights!

www.ingramcontent.com/pod-product-compliance
Lightning Source LLC
Chambersburg PA
CBHW071324120626
46546CB00002B/428

* 9 7 8 1 9 6 5 4 0 1 2 5 5 *